# Feeling Your Way Along

# Feeling Your Way Along

## Using Your Emotions as a Pathway to Enlightenment

by

**Stephen BE**
**with Donna BE**

**BEing There Publications**™
Grand Junction, Colorado USA

# *Feeling Your Way Along*

## Using Your Emotions As A Pathway To Enlightenment
by
Stephen BE with Donna BE

Published by
BEing There Publications™,
a division of
BEing There Enlightenment Systems, Inc.
650 Main Street, Suite 2
Grand Junction, Colorado 81501  USA
Tel. (toll free) 1-800-598-0370    Tel. (local) 970-245-6502
Fax 970-434-2967
E-mail: frontdesk@BTES.com    Website: www.BTES.com

**First Edition**

**Library of Congress Preassigned Card Number: 99-090899**
BE, Stephen B.
    *Feeling* Your Way Along
    Using Your Emotions As A Pathway To Enlightenment - 1st Ed.
  /   Stephen BE (1951- ) with Donna BE (1951- )

ISBN 1-929739-01-X

# Dedication

This book is dedicated to all the millions of people who have used psychotherapy as a tool for their personal growth, regardless of what motivated you to seek professional counseling.

The authors salute your courage in being willing to look at yourself, your perseverance in being willing to live with your initial discomfort long enough to enjoy the unfolding, the level of self-responsibility you claim, and your commitment to your personal truth as you create a conscious reality.

Willingness, courage, perseverance, tenacity, patience and commitment are characteristics necessary to experience higher levels of consciousness. From these are born the seeds of enlightenment. Namaste.

SB & DB

## Acknowledgement

The authors wish to express their humble gratitude to
Deborah A. Hackett, MD, and Peter H. Hackett, MD,
who's faith, encouragement, and support
nurtured this project to fruition.

# *Feeling Your Way Along*

## Using Your Emotions As A Pathway To Enlightenment

## Contents

# Preface
# Higher Consciousness

*C*onsciousness is the way in which we experience the world. We have the ability to develop our consciousness. Its level of development is determined by the skill levels of the four aspects of BEing: physical, mental, emotional, spiritual. All four aspects of BEing are equally important, and skills must be progressed on all four aspects.

Even though most individuals are very skilled on one or two of their aspects, it is the skill level that is common to all four aspects that determines their Level of Consciousness. The limiting aspect will always be the aspect of least development.

For most people, their emotional aspect is the aspect of least development. Therefore, it is the determining factor in their Level of Consciousness. This is true simply because very few people ever receive training in their emotional aspect. Physical training and mental training are abundant in the western societies. Spiritual training is acknowledged and addressed, even if not sufficiently. The emotional aspect is largely ignored in western society, leaving most people untrained.

When you learn and practice emotional skills, you grow in consciousness. Growth will continue up to the aspect with the next lowest skill level. Then the skills of that aspect must be addressed. Higher Levels of Consciousness are available to everyone who learns and practices the skills of higher levels, regardless of education, economics, race, religion, gender, or gross measures of ability in physical, mental or spiritual aspects.

Lower Levels of Consciousness create a world dominated by matters of security, sensation, and power. These levels are driven by the emotional skill of denial, with the purpose of survival.

Higher levels create a world where you experience intimacy, unity, union, and enlightenment. If you want to experience intimacy, you must learn and practice the skills of that Level of Consciousness. You create the world you live in by the Level of Consciousness you practice. "Consciousness precedes BEing." (Vaclav Havel)

BEing There Enlightenment Systems helps you learn the skills of consciousness.

▲

## Introduction

his is an instruction manual. It introduces the tools you must have to be able to use your emotions effectively. This means being able to use every one of your emotional experiences to uncover, identify, clarify, and if necessary, update the part of you that provides perfect guidance for your personal growth into higher levels of consciousness, and eventually, enlightenment.

Your level of consciousness is what determines your experiences in life. Depending upon the consciousness you practice, you create experiences that are consistent with that level of consciousness. For example, if you practice the Security Level of Consciousness, you will be preoccupied with matters of security, and all of your experiences will be reflections of your reality. Similarly, if you wish to experience intimacy in your primary relationships, then you must be practicing that level of consciousness.

Level of consciousness, however, is not an arbitrary choice. Your level of consciousness must, and will, reflect what is true for you. Your inner truth is not, usually, readily evident. You must seek to discover your truth, to bring it into your conscious awareness. This can only be accomplished through your emotions, as your personal truth can only be experienced emotionally.

Seeking your personal truth is full-time work. You cannot dabble in the pursuit of truth, and expect it to be available to you when you need it to be able to make conscious choices in your behavior. To have your personal truth to guide your choices in your life is the essence of personal power. It is what gives your life true purpose. It defines a life well spent, versus a life of lower consciousness pursuits. Living in accordance with your personal truth is what allows you to create true intimacy in your life. It allows you to move beyond the petty pursuits of security, sensation and power.

Living in truth and seeking higher consciousness are lofty goals to pursue. They will require many years of personal exploration and inner work. However, the pursuit must start from humble beginnings. The pursuit of higher consciousness must always begin with acquiring emotional skills. When you practice your emotional skills faithfully, you will directly encounter the lessons you need to learn in order to grow into higher levels consciousness.

*Feeling* **Your Way Along** provides a foundation for any self-exploration you may do, whether it be under the guidance of a psychotherapist, or self-directed. Eventually, everyone needs to use counseling to seek and deal with his or her growth issues. Emotional skills are only taught in therapy. There is no other environment where you can learn these skills. **FYWA** will introduce the tools you need, but it is in counseling that you will learn the skills to use these tools well.

If a therapist cannot offer you guidance in your self-discovery, then he or she is not going to be very helpful, and you should seek a more skillful therapist. It is akin to hiring someone to guide you through the wilderness. It behooves you to find someone who is familiar with the territory, someone who can show you through the passes, someone who can inform you of the dangers. Obviously it is not up to the therapist to decide upon your destination. But it is their job to help you find the most helpful route to get there, by pointing out the choices available to you along the way.

If a therapist merely nods, and utters an occasional "uh-huh", find a more skillful therapist, who can teach and guide. Find someone who can engage with you and who models these skills in his or her own life. Like all professions, there are bad therapists, mediocre therapists, and good therapists. Keep searching until you find a therapist that can teach you how to discover and claim what is true for you.

The authors wish to make this presentation a very personal one. Their use of the second person, you, fosters this personal connection. This also minimizes the awkwardness of the English language in stating things in gender-neutral terminology. When necessary, "his" and "her" are used randomly, maintaining consistency only within the confines of the thought being presented.

*Italics are used throughout this presentation to highlight words that describe emotional experience.* When learning the skills of emotions, it is necessary to expand your vocabulary for emotions. Pay particular attention to these words, and try to identify your experience that defines these words. In other words, do not settle for this merely as an intellectual endeavor. Attempt to make it an emotional one. Question. Wonder. But most of all, feel. Emotions are your birthright. They are what make you human. They are the source of your personal power. They are your guidance system for finding your way home.

▲

Stephen BE and Donna BE

# PART I: The Foundation

# Chapter 1
# The Wisdom of Emotions

*N*ot only is every emotion okay to feel, emotions provide an internal guidance system, available to everyone, that can lead you through *confusion, chaos, perplexity, pain,* and *darkness,* to your enlightenment. In order for the guidance system to work, however, <u>every emotion must be felt</u>. Then it must be worked with, and then it must be channeled into deliberate behavior. The emotion is available for you to use effectively to realize higher levels of consciousness and to deliberately create what you truly want. Emotion is always available. Whether you work with it effectively, or not, is a matter of choice and skill.

Emotions are your energy, your alarm system, and your motivating force. Emotions provide your ability to connect to other people, your sense of purpose, and your guiding light. Emotions give you access to your personal power, and they provide a failsafe system for measuring truth. Emotions indicate the work you need to do, and they are the reward for having done it. Emotions are the essence of everything you ever *hope* for, and the core of everything you *fear.*

Emotions are the key to your awareness. In fact, unless you feel about something, you remain unaware of it. There are an infinite number of events occurring constantly. Of these, you become aware of only a few. Your awareness of any event is brought about by your emotional experience. Things only exist to you if you feel about them.

For example, you may have read the morning newspaper thoroughly. But the only information that registered in your awareness is that which triggered an emotion. Maybe you felt *interested* in a certain topic. Perhaps you *wondered* if a recent development would affect you. A certain report might have invited *irritation* or *anger.* You may have immediately denied the emotion, but the emotion was already there. It was emotion that gave the event energy and made it real to you.

Emotions are the motivating force in life. They are what give energy to everything you think and do. Emotion has been with you since before you were born. Emotions permeate every occurrence in every moment of your life. Like ether that surrounds you, you constantly live in the middle of emotional energy. Emotions are so ever-present, that they become invisible. Emotions, largely, go as unnoticed as the air you breathe. Surrounded by them; engulfed by them; permeated by them; driven by them; yet almost always unnoticed.

Emotions have an impeccable, if not divine, wisdom about them. They bring into your direct awareness the lessons you need to address in order to grow into higher consciousness. Emotions are the not-too-subtle clues that the universe has been giving you about your real purpose in life. Not making money; not accomplishing great things; definitely not to propagate or improve the species; you were born for the sole purpose of learning how to reconnect to the divine source. God, universal consciousness, unity with all things, the Tao, universal essence, enlightenment, whatever name you wish to give it; emotions are the homing device to bring you there.

To make emotions work for you, you must allow them to exist freely. You must BE free of intent to deny them, manipulate them, avoid them, project them, suppress them, delay them, or hide them. You will begin to BE free when you allow your emotions to exist, unaffected by your judgment, and disconnected from your inclinations to behave in certain ways, otherwise known as your reactions.

BEing is a state of being in which your emotions exist, unfettered and fully available, for your use in claiming higher consciousness. Each emotion must be embraced, explored, and put into deliberate use. Emotions are not a sign of human failure. They are the sign of human being, and when used effectively, human BEing. Emotions are the key to your BEing.

You must learn emotional skills however, to know how to work effectively with your emotions. BEing requires that you learn how to use your emotional capacity, at all times. And using your emotional capacity first requires that you be fully aware, without prejudice, of what you feel.

As you read these sentences, no performance is required. There is no reward for reading these passages quickly. There is no behavior that is immediately required. If you are not allowing them to touch you, to sink in and affect your experience, then you are not BEing. Start now to learn the skills necessary for BEing. Without screening for emotions you don't want to feel, or wish you wouldn't feel, or believe you never feel, go inside yourself to feel what you truly feel.

What are you feeling right now? *Bored? Annoyed? Impatient? Inquisitive? Eager? Open? Loving? Lonely?* Stop long enough, right now, to feel how you feel. Try to tune in to these ever-present messages. Try to notice the emotional energy of your being. Do you feel *agitation? Comfort? Satisfaction? Joy? Superior? Righteous? Sad?*

Do you recognize your feelings? Can you allow them to occur within yourself, without judgment? Can you feel deeply? Do you recognize the various layers of emotion that are happening right now inside you? If you cannot identify how you feel right now, then you are missing this divine source of guidance inherent in your BEing. Without a map, arriving at your destination can be very difficult.

If your sole purpose in life is to reconnect with your divine source, then it must be true that you would be aware of this experience when it finally occurs. Otherwise, you might just go right past the experience without knowing you did what you needed to do. In other words, your consciousness will recognize the experience of reconnection, or enlightenment. Consciousness is how you know what you know, or know what you experience. Consciousness is the way in which you experience the world.

You have the ability to develop your consciousness. Doing so requires skill. Your Level of Consciousness is determined by the skill levels of the four aspects of BEing: physical, mental, emotional, spiritual. All four aspects of BEing are equally important, and skills must be progressed on all four aspects.

Even though you are probably very skilled on one or two of your aspects, it is the skill level that is common to all four aspects that determines your Level of Consciousness. The limiting aspect will always be the aspect of least development.

For most people, the emotional aspect is the aspect of least development. Therefore, it is the determining factor in their Level of Consciousness. This is true simply because very few people ever receive training in their emotional aspect. Physical training and mental training are abundant in the western societies. Spiritual training is acknowledged and addressed, even if not sufficiently. The emotional aspect is largely ignored in western society, leaving most people untrained.

Consider all of your education and training. If you participated in an American educational system, you probably learned much about reading, and writing, and arithmetic. Perhaps you learned about science, history, geography, higher mathematics and languages. If you had a superior education, you might have studied literature, and art, and business, and technology. A college education may have taken you to great depths in any of these areas. And professional training might have exhausted the amount of knowledge available in that area up to that moment.

Whether ten years, twelve years or twenty-five years of education, how much guidance did you receive in the area of emotions? Did anyone tell you what an emotion is, or how to use them to access your truth, or how to use them to create what you truly want? Did anyone tell you that relationships are built on emotion, or how to use your emotions to create the kinds of relationships you would like to have? The most important things in anyone's life are founded in emotion: marriage, parent-child relationships, success, growth, satisfaction and purpose. These are all founded in emotion, yet for most people, there was little or no education in this aspect.

There is a gross assumption that when you reach a certain age, it becomes your turn to go out into the world to marry, to create children, and to succeed in life. But no one tells you how! It is testimony to the human spirit that people continue to try, even without having adequate skills. It shouldn't shock anyone that, in a society where adults have free choice, 50% of all marriages end in divorce. It's even more surprising that 50% choose to continue trying, even though their Level of Consciousness will allow them only the emotional experiences of the lower levels.

Lower Levels of Consciousness create a world dominated by matters of security, sensation, and power. These levels are driven by the emotional skill of denial, with the purpose of survival.

When you learn and practice emotional skills, you grow in consciousness. Growth will continue up to the aspect with the next lowest skill level. Then the skills of that aspect must be addressed, along with continued emotional lessons. Higher Levels of Consciousness are available to everyone who learns and practices the skills of higher levels, regardless of education, economics, race, religion, gender, or gross measures of ability in physical, mental or spiritual aspects.

Higher levels create a world where you experience intimacy, unity, union, and enlightenment. If you want to experience intimacy, you must learn and practice the skills of that Level of Consciousness. It is the conscious experience of intimacy that indicates your success at having realized this Level of Consciousness. If you were not experiencing intimacy, and the other emotions found at the Intimacy Level of Consciousness, it would be presumptuous to think you had achieved that level.

Similarly, if you do not experience the emotions found at even higher levels of consciousness, such as unity and union, then your claim of that level of consciousness would not ring true. Enlightenment is realized when you have the conscious experience, emotionally, of enlightenment. You create the world you live in by the Level of Consciousness you practice. And consciousness is claimed through the acquisition and execution of emotional skills. "Consciousness precedes BEing."

> " *Consciousness precedes BEing.* "
> (Vaclav Havel)

Consciousness is not thinking. Thinking is a skill on the mental aspect of BEing. It is a useful skill, and a necessary one for development on the mental aspect. Consciousness is the level of development that is common to all four aspects: the physical, spiritual and emotional aspects, as well as the mental aspect.

How many ways have you heard the message that you are wrong to feel certain emotions? "Get rid of sadness." "Quit being negative." "Why so glum? Put on a smile." The standard message about emotion is to think more positively, as though thinking will overrule your emotions. In valuing and practicing thinking, you are taught that you will have some sense of *control* in your life. Whereas, allowing yourself to feel whatever you feel is equated to being out of control. You probably have heard and been taught that if you could only think differently, then you could do something about your emotional state. Then you would feel differently.

Enormous amounts of time and money are spent in an effort to learn to think differently. "Be more positive!" "Think positively!" "Accentuate the positive, eliminate the negative!" "The power of positive thinking!" "Personal power from positive affirmations!" "Improve your attitude." "Only winners wanted around here." "Believe it and it can happen." And so on. There are hundreds of books and courses devoted to the concept that "how you feel is a result of how you think."

This simply is not so! There is thinking. And there is feeling. They are different. They are not disconnected altogether, but they are different aspects of your BEing. This is the first lesson about emotions. While thinking and emotions can reflect each other, thinking does not cause your emotions. One is not better than the other, merely different.

Like the right hand is different than the left hand, they each have value, they each have strengths. Your greatest personal power is summoned when you learn to use them both together.

If you went about your life as though you had only a right arm and no left arm, you would naturally try to avoid those activities that required use of your left arm. Even if you did acknowledge the presence of such a left arm, you would know it was of no real use. For it would be weak and unreliable from atrophy. You would avoid having to call on this undeveloped left arm for anything but the simplest involvement.

Emotions, especially unpleasant emotions, are often regarded as inconvenient annoyances. Instead of celebrating their potential, you prefer they would go away, never to return. The pleasant emotions are greeted with acceptance and expectation. Or perhaps those, too, are regarded with suspicion and wariness. A "thinking" person certainly doesn't want to be seduced by pleasurable emotions. Even when you feel "good" emotions, you might not indulge yourself. Your skill in using your emotions effectively, therefore, remains undeveloped and weak. Your emotional aspect is unreliable, and something to be avoided as being of no real use; or even denied.

There is value to training your mind to think in a disciplined way when you are striving for some form of maximum performance. Performance, which means doing very specific behaviors in a very deliberate fashion, is necessary to achieve some goals. But performance is not the key to your most important issues in life, such as marriage, raising children, and fulfilling your purpose. For these issues you must learn how to BE; how to BE in a marriage; how to BE a parent; how to BE yourself. "BEing" is a very different undertaking from "doing." "Doing" is more important than "BEing" only when your survival is threatened. It is generally ineffective for everyday use.

Learning to think well does not change the way you feel. You merely focus your ability in a different aspect. Instead of reacting irrationally, you can apply the discipline of thought to your decision-making process. You still feel the same emotions, but now you have a sense of being in *control*. While thinking allows you to live with more *confidence* in your ability to survive, you are still living at the Security Level of Consciousness.

Living life at the Security Level of Consciousness, level one, even if mental discipline is applied to your emotions, demands certain attitudes within yourself. You must train yourself to encourage certain perceptions, and to discourage certain distractions. You think you can't afford to feel certain feelings. Because you think, you applaud your superior way of BEing. You think you're BEing smart, living with your eyes wide open.

Your vigilance level for emotions that might overpower your disciplined thinking must necessarily be high. You think you're not just reacting to situations as they arise. You're always watching for who or what is going to try next to "get" you, thinking that if you can see it coming you are better able to use your mental aspect to deal with it. You can't afford to let yourself *trust* too much. You can't get too close to anyone, for then they might "really get" you. You live your life in constant *ambivalence* over whether to get closer or farther apart from those around you. If you perceive someone as *betraying* your *trust* you tend to chastise yourself for *trusting* too much. Your emotions are regarded as *annoying, interrupting, inefficient, misleading,* and even *dangerous.* So you constantly strive to minimize your emotional experiences. Then you wonder why your relationships are "luke-warm", at best, or your life has no real purpose, or *satisfaction* and *contentment* are absent.

These are the prices you pay for continuing to live in the Security Level of Consciousness. You never develop any real *intimacy*, despite the longevity of your relationships. At best, in general reference to your life, you are *lonely* or *dependent, impatient, unhappy, unfulfilled,* and *dissatisfied* despite any outward appearances of success; "a life," as H. D. Thoreau described, of "quiet *desperation*." At worst, you feel *lost, depressed* or *anxious* most of the time; perhaps even to the point of wondering "what's the point of going on like this, there must be more to life." The more you practice your mental discipline, in an effort to control or suppress your emotions, the worse you feel. You know what's wrong. You can feel it. You just don't know how to make it right.

Allow yourself to feel right now. *Angry? Frightened? Alone? Misunderstood? Validated?* Are you *afraid* to experience your emotions? What might happen if you tuned-in to how you really feel right now? Are you *afraid* someone around you might see how you feel? If they did, would you then feel *vulnerable* to them? Would they see your *anger*, your *fear*, your *rage*, your *loneliness*, your *sadness*, your tears?

What if they did see you as you really are right now? Would you then *suffer embarrassment, or fear of being misunderstood* or *judge*d, or some other emotion you are actively avoiding? Are you *afraid* you might get *caught-up* or *lost* in your emotion, and then you wouldn't be able to do the things you were planning to do? Avoiding emotional experience, of any flavor, keeps you locked in your Security Level of Consciousness, continuing to do the same old behaviors and hoping for different results.

BEing allows, and requires, you to feel whatever you feel in each and every moment. When you are BEing, you do not pretend you are not feeling, that you do not have emotions. When you are BEing, you do not try to avoid certain emotional experiences. Instead, you learn to draw upon the strength that comes from your emotions. By making more conscious decisions about your actions in every moment, you move away from the Security Level, and into higher Levels of Consciousness. It is only there that you find the ability to create your life consciously.

At higher consciousness, the world is not out to get you. You can quit wasting your energy on *vigilance*, *ambivalence*, and *defensiveness*. The world becomes a reflection of your creation, in which, instead of quiet *desperation*, you take quiet *enjoyment*. BEing.

"But," you might argue to yourself, "to feel in each and every moment means to acknowledge feelings and situations which you do not know how to handle, or they take too much time to deal with in an already overloaded schedule." Immediately you are confronted with the situations of your daily life: the spouse with whom you have frequent arguments or perhaps even feel little or no *love*; the child who questions your authority; the employer who *disrespects* and *takes advantage* of you; the friend who never seems to be there. Then it gets even more *intimidating*. The impossible global situations come into your awareness: racial, religious and ethnic *prejudice*; *injustice*; starvation; poverty; subjugation. Who could possibly function if they allowed themselves to feel all that? Or so you argue to justify your avoidance and denial.

At your Security Level of Consciousness, where "doing" takes precedence over "BEing", you think if you feel certain emotions you must then act upon them. Hence you avoid emotions that seem futile. "After all," you tell yourself, "how can I really change starvation (prejudice, injustice, etc.) in the world." So you do what you can to avoid feeling those feelings of *sympathy*, *outrage*, *compassion*, and *responsibility*. You try to take a part of your awareness and suppress it. Since you cannot "do" anything about your feeling, you just won't feel it. You exercise your mental discipline to reduce or eliminate your awareness of these emotional experiences.

Your mind tricks you into believing you need your thinking to survive, even when you're really not in a survival situation. Are these situations happening right now in your present experience? Are you starving right now? Are you experiencing *prejudice* right now? Are you receiving *injustice* right now? Right now, in this moment? If you were, you probably wouldn't be reading this. These experiences are real, and they do exist somewhere right now. They may be just out of your present moment. Perhaps they were your experience just moments ago, before you were reading. Or perhaps you anticipate they will occur again soon, and perhaps often. But how do you feel right now? This is not a survival situation. Nor are most of the situations in your life.

BEing requires you to learn to focus your attention to the moment at hand, right here and right now. What are you feeling? You can't be fooled by your survival consciousness into thinking that you can do anything about the past moments or the future moments. The only moment you have any effect on is the one that is with you right now. And in order to affect it consciously, you must be fully present.    BEing.

Emotions are the key to BEing. Claim your emotions and the personal power they provide, then you are able to make conscious decisions in every moment of your life. But if you deny your emotions, any of your emotions, you squander away your personal power, the power to create your life consciously. You relegate yourself to living unconsciously.

You may continue to applaud your ability to think, even as you continue your unconscious life. You then suffer the consequences of choices you made, not through conscious choice, but through unconscious reaction. You must. For all situations in life arise from choices you made previously. You are not in complete control of every occurrence. You do not control the choices of others. Your choices, however, bring you to the table of life.

As an example, you may have been hit by a bus. You certainly didn't have any control over the bus. But you chose to put yourself in the place where buses can travel.

How you make your choices in your life dictate whether you can see your responsibility ahead of time. If you accept your responsibility for your choices, then you can accept the consequences of having made that choice, even if you get hit by a bus. If you know ahead of time that making a certain choice may put you in the path of an on-coming bus, then you will probably be very deliberate in making such a choice.

Thinking cannot give you this information. Thinking helps, no doubt. Sophisticated and disciplined thinking may provide you with much information. The more information, and the better the thinking process, the better you will anticipate possible consequences to your choices.

But your fate is not dictated by your ability to predict the future.

It is determined by your ability to claim full responsibility for yourself right now. If you can claim full responsibility for the choices you make now, then it becomes far easier to accept the myriad variables of situations that emerge from that path.

Claiming responsibility for your choices is easier said than done. Responsibility involves much more than merely proclaiming "I'll cross that bridge when I get to it," or "the chances of that happening are negligible." If, when you get to the "worst case scenario," you defend your choices with "if I had known this was going to happen ...", then you have not claimed your responsibility for your choice.

Responsibility is an emotional skill. It is not a statement of your character. It is not a measure of your strength, or mental attitude, or physical prowess. Responsibility is not about how much education you have had, at least not in the conventional sense of the term. It is not about your monetary choices. It is not a judgment about your civic pride. Responsibility is not what is displayed when you take care of other people. It is not about how well you can suppress your needs or desires. It most definitely is not what is displayed when you tolerate high levels of emotional pain, or mental or physical pain.

Responsibility for self is learned, and learned, and learned some more. It requires a lifetime of learning to claim more and more of your responsibility. Emotional skills are required to learn how to claim your responsibility, without taking responsibility that is not yours. Responsibility skills are the key to changing your Level of Consciousness, so that you are not maintaining a life that is driven by survival.

When you know what to claim responsibility for, and how to claim it, you open up an inner link to a source of wisdom not previously available. You can feel the natural rhythm of the world, the energy that flows through all things, the sense of connection that defines faith. From this inner wisdom, you have a sense of Knowing, as opposed to merely knowing. It's an experience of *certainty*, and *groundedness*, and *clarity*. It is the difference between doing something because you think it is a good idea, and doing something because it is in alignment with your inner truth.

With this internal guidance system, your choices become based in the experience of Knowing everything there is to know about yourself at that moment: how it got there, what the effects have been, how it drives you, what's important to you, how you tend to see things and events in the world, and so on. This is the experience of Knowing what is true for you right now. What is true for you may or may not be true for anybody else. It really doesn't matter. Claiming self-responsibility means claiming your personal truth in the face of all odds. Like Mohandas Gandhi said, "Even in a minority of one, the truth is still the truth."

Emotions provide you access to your personal truth. You must be able to feel your way to this inner truth. It is not accessible any other way. You cannot think your way there. You cannot pray your way there. You cannot force yourself physically to BE there. All of the skills of the other three aspects of BEing are useful, and necessary, in realizing greater consciousness. But access to your personal truth is provided only by your emotions. If you are unaware of your emotions, or lack the skill to use them, you do not have access to your personal truth.

Connect to and claim your truth in every moment, and you have the ability to make conscious choices. If you do not claim your truth in every moment, you do not have this capability. Conscious choices are the only means of creating your world so that it reflects your truth. Emotions are the key to creating a conscious world. What are you feeling right now? And right now? And now? And now? And right now? ....

Every time you feel an emotion, you have a path being opened up to your truth. Following that path means allowing yourself to feel your emotions as they occur. You literally feel your way along the path to your truth. Enlightenment is realized by **feeling your way along** the path, laid out by your emotions, to your personal truth.

But in order to feel your way along, you must acquire new tools to work with your emotions; and then practice the skills necessary to use those tools well. If emotions, in the past, *scared* you or *repulsed* you or *enamored* you or *excited* you or *annoyed* you, it was only because you lacked the proper tools to work with them effectively. Nothing makes a job more difficult than not having the right tools for that job.

Emotional tools are no different. You must have the right tools and the right skills to use those tools. You wouldn't automatically know these skills, and you wouldn't have the tools, unless you specifically sought them. They are counter-intuitive, and they are largely unavailable to most people. Intelligence plays no role in knowing them. Education, unless it was specific education in the emotional skills, is irrelevant. Religious, racial, ethnic, gender, physical and financial differences are moot.

In order to work with your emotions there are four concepts, or constructs, that everyone must know. These constructs, together, form a foundation upon which emotional skills can be acquired and practiced.

The constructs form a framework for understanding and accepting emotions, and learning how to welcome them as opportunities to access your personal truth.

Each piece of the foundation must be fully integrated before moving on to the next. And they must be re-visited regularly to assure deeper understanding and integration. These foundation constructs are presented in the next four chapters. Then the emotional tools and the skills to use them will follow in Part II.

Emotions are your source of wisdom. Emotions are how you experience the world around you. They are what create awareness. Emotions are your only access to your personal truth. And when you use them to update your truth and claim responsibility for your truth, they become a source of personal power. They allow you to choose your behavior consciously, thereby creating a world that reflects your truth. This brings you to a higher level of consciousness and a world that differs from the one of lower consciousness. All this comes from your emotions, but only if you allow them to BE.

▲

# Chapter 2
# The Unconscious
# (Construct #1)

*T*he first of the foundation constructs is the understanding that you are much more than you think you are. If you were asked "Who are you," you could answer the question in great detail. You might speak your name, your history, your memories, your accomplishments, your relationships, your physical description, your goals, your beliefs, your desires, your thoughts, your education, your family, your chosen work, etc. Your answer to this question could conceivably fill volumes, if you were exhaustive.

Yet, even if you were thorough in your description, all that you could verbalize would constitute only a small part of who you are. For everything that you can verbalize in response to this question is the part of you of which you are conscious. There is another part that exists outside of your consciousness that is called your unconscious.

The unconscious is the part of you that urges you to survive. Processed in the brain stem and the limbic lobes of the brain, the unconscious registers in the part of your brain that houses your fight-or-flight response to threatening situations. The *rage* that is registered in your limbic lobes, located just behind your ears, enables you to create the adrenaline necessary to run fast enough to get away or to fight as though your life depended on it.

There are two characteristics of the unconscious that make it significant in understanding your emotions. The first is that its sole purpose is to guarantee your survival. The unconscious has a radar-like ability to perceive threat, and then sound the alarm. It provides a screening device that measures the safety of all incoming stimuli. Anything that you perceive, through any of your senses, gets routed through this screen to determine whether or not it is a safe event. If a stimulus is perceived as safe, it passes through the screen into your more sophisticated perceptual abilities. If the stimulus is perceived as not safe, then your limbic lobes go into a ready state for fight-or-flight.

The second characteristic is that, in the unconscious, there is no time. There is no linear progression from past to present to future. It is all one moment in the unconscious. Whatever was, is now, and always will be. This characteristic becomes especially important when you begin to consider the effects of your childhood on your emotions.

The evidence of the unconscious can be observed. We know of its presence through observation of word usage, body language, word association, deja vu experiences, Rorschach and other projective tests, stream-of-consciousness talk or journaling, dreams, parenting messages we employ, and other subjective signs. Since the unconscious by definition is outside of your consciousness, it is difficult to measure its size. But we know it is present, and we know it is influencing how you perceive and react to the world around you. If you are to achieve mastery in your life, you must learn to see your unconscious, and learn how to use it effectively.

To understand your unconscious, you need to go back to the beginning, the beginning of your life. It is here that the unconscious is programmed to perceive and react to guarantee your survival. There is ample evidence that the unconscious is learning to perceive and react while the child is still inside the mother's womb. But at what point this occurs in development, or if it is consistent among developing fetuses, is not yet known. So it is convenient to use birth as a starting point.

When you were in your mother's womb, you experienced perfection. You had no needs, since the instant a need arose it was satisfied. You did not experience hunger; you were continuously being nourished. You did not feel too hot or too cold; this was a temperature-controlled environment. Auditory and tactile stimuli were muffled by the softness of your surrounding. You heard the constant sound of your mother's heartbeat, and experienced the rhythm of life. The highly respected marriage therapist and author, Harville Hendrix, describes this state as "original wholeness,"[1] and cites the Jewish theologian, Martin Buber, who refers to "fetal existence, [as] communion with the universe."

This perfection came to a violent and abrupt end with the experience of maternal labor. Most adults can *sympathize, empathize,* and/or *respect* the work a woman does to birth a child. Imagine this experience as an infant, who is being evicted from its perfect home. After hours of intense discomfort, the child is introduced into a world that often treats it roughly, and is cold and harsh. For the first time it experiences lack; first it is lack of oxygen, then lack of comfort, lack of food, and lack of nurturance.

With each experience of lack the infant is confronting the new reality, called "need". By definition, a need is not met right now. Even if the need is met as soon as the caregivers realize what it is, the infant has

---

[1] Hendrix, Harville. <u>Getting The Love You Need; A Guide For Couples</u>, Henry Holt & Company, New York, 1998. p.14.

already experienced the need. Each new need is experienced as a threat to its survival. In that moment of need, that is all the infant knows.

There is no remembrance of needs being successfully met. The child has no ability to postpone the need, or mitigate the need, or assuage it by telling themselves, "I know they will get to me as soon as they can." There is no past, no future; only the eternal now moment in which the child is experiencing need.

In that infantile state, a need is not just a temporary experience of discomfort. It is an eternal confrontation with death. If an infant is hungry, its reality is that it is in the act of dying. If the infant needs nurturing, its organism knows it must receive it in order to avoid death. If it is too cold, it is confronting death. And so it continues with each need.

Since the infant is separate from its mother, it needs life-ensuring things that, by definition, are not automatically fulfilled. Being entirely dependent upon others, someone else must do something to care for the infant. That task falls to the parents, or primary caretakers.

As anyone who has raised a child knows, an infant is a never-ending cycle of needs. They wake up and need to have their clothing changed to eliminate the skin irritation caused by urine or feces. They need to be fed, nurtured, stimulated, bathed, fed again, and laid to rest. The parent may have a short respite, and then it starts all over again.

There is virtually no way a parent can fulfill all of the needs a child may experience. This is true no matter how loving and doting a parent may be. A parent may take five minutes to wake up to the sound of a hunger cry from their infant, for example. During those five minutes the child is confronted with having an eternal need (no "time" in the unconscious) that threatens their survival (faced with death). Every child experiences needs that are unmet, for however long a duration that may be. These unmet needs create imprints in the unconscious.

This continues from the moment of birth, day after day, month after month, year after year, until the child begins to take on some of the responsibility of meeting its own needs. Somewhere around the age of 6, the child begins to claim an identity separate from the mother and father (or primary caretakers, when these are not the parents).

They no longer experience themselves as just another appendage of their parents; like another arm or another leg. The child can begin to meet some of her own needs: fix a sandwich, dress herself, nurture herself, etc. This is the age of consciousness. It is celebrated in many cultures as a point of awakening. Children usually begin school at this age. They receive religious sacraments. Their acculturation begins in earnest.

From this time forward the child has an increasing ability to screen incoming data through his own understanding of himself. He can moderate the urgency of his needs with his concept of time: "I'm hungry now, but I know I will be fed in a little while." He is able to begin to utilize his understanding of human frailty: "Dad was just tired and frustrated about the car not working. He is not really mad at me." His consciousness thus moderates his needs; turning off the survival alarm that occurs unconsciously.

Before the emergence of consciousness, with its moderating effect, all experiences of the child are registered directly in the unconscious. This is called imprinting. The process of imprinting can be understood by picturing the unconscious as a block of modeling clay, and every experience the child has imprints on that clay. The clay gets molded by being pushed here and pressed there. Experiences do not add to, nor take away from, the amount of clay. They just shape what is already there, permanently.

Because the unconscious inherited a purpose to guarantee survival, those events in the child's life that threaten its survival leave a more significant imprint in the unconscious. Events such as hunger, isolation, pain, temperature discomfort, and so on, stir the unconscious and leave an imprint.

Experiences such as *rejection, invalidation, judgment, frustration,* etc., are also perceived by the child's unconscious as threats to survival. The relationships upon which he depends for his survival are under threat. When the severity of these events and experiences is increased, the imprint is more significant.

It is a sad fact of life that not all parents are loving and doting to their infant children. Severe treatment of children creates more severe imprinting. When a child suffers physical or sexual abuse, or neglect, she will experience the effects forever in her life. The imprints created by such experiences are like full-force, fist-like blows to the modeling clay of the unconscious. The frequency and degree to which a child must confront death is what determines the problems she will be confronting throughout her life.

The child's unconscious is also affected by pleasurable events. But since these generally do not involve a survival response, they do not create as significant an imprint. The absence of imprinting, in this model, is a virtue. It is when a child is less severely imprinted that he enjoys more *wholeness, peace, happiness, love, wonder, awe,* and all the other experiences of health. It is the unique way in which a child's unconscious is imprinted, with both pleasurable and threatening experiences, that creates much of his personality.

The exact proportion of consciousness to unconscious is not known. It may vary from one person to another. While the unconscious can be observed, it cannot be measured by current means. What we know is that it is helpful to allow it a generous amount of respect. In coming to know yourself fully, it is more useful to over-estimate the effect of your unconscious than it is to under-estimate it.

In <u>Getting the Love You Want</u>[2], Harville Hendrix explains the scope of the unconscious in terms of stars in the night sky. He invites you to imagine that if you live in a city and look up at the night sky, you might see a few stars. You might know there are probably more of them up there, but because of interference from surrounding lights you can't see them. If you could leave the city and look at the sky from smaller towns, then you would see many more stars in the sky; perhaps hundreds. If you could go further out into the countryside, where the interference from surrounding light is eliminated, you would be amazed at the thousands of stars you could now see in the night sky. And if you were lucky enough to be able to sit on a mountain on a summer night, you would experience "millions" of stars in the sky!

The stars were always there. It was only because you changed your perspective that you were able to see them. Such is the lesson of the unconscious: you must change your perspective to be able to see what was always there, and especially to see it in its immensity.

Consider an iceberg floating in an ocean. No matter how big the portion of the iceberg that shows above the surface may be, there is always another 89% of the total mass of that iceberg that is below the surface of the water. Your consciousness may be represented by the 11% of the iceberg that is above the surface, and your unconscious by the 89% below the surface.

As much as you would like to think you are in conscious control of your life, this just does not prove to be true. Your unconscious is your driving mass, by far; just as the 89% of the iceberg below the surface is its driving mass.

Imagine if you could get in a boat and row out to that iceberg. And when you reached it, you could step out onto that iceberg, right at water level. If you looked up and surveyed the iceberg you might be

---

[2] Hendrix, Ibid., p.8.

impressed with its size. You might know that there has to be something in the water that holds up so much mass, and you might even see some of what is below the surface. But your attention would be drawn to the more obviously visible part above the surface.

If you were surveying your consciousness in this manner, you would be duly impressed with all that you know about yourself. You might have some appreciation for whatever it is below the surface that holds up this mass of consciousness. But you wouldn't yet know what it is, nor be able to see it.

If you climbed part way up the iceberg, you would gain a new perspective. From here you would be able to see back down through the surface of the water to notice the bulk below the surface. You would see how it is shaped, how it sticks out very far in some directions, but not in others, and so on. Your *appreciation* for the below-surface mass would increase. You would know it was a significant part and could not be ignored in total assessment.

If you went all the way to the peak of this iceberg and again looked back through the surface, you would notice that your perspective had changed significantly. Now you could see all of the specifics and peculiarities of the below-surface portion. You would fully *appreciate* its sheer mass. You might begin to understand, no matter how hard you tried to direct the path of the iceberg, something else always seemed to be happening. You could see why the iceberg could not be moved close to another iceberg; it sticks out very far in that direction under the surface, so there was always a rub.

You might not ever be able to see all that makes up your unconscious. The iceberg has an underside, which is not visible from above, no matter how high you climb. But the ability to recognize your unconscious, gives you the opportunity to work with it. If you know that the iceberg sticks out a great distance on one side, then before you try to bring it in contact with another iceberg, you can re-orient so that you increase your chances of getting what you truly want.

This is perhaps the greatest of all the constructs. To know that you have an unconscious part of you, as well as a conscious part, and to know how to work with your unconscious, gives you the ability to understand how you create your world.

▲

# Chapter 3
# The Pyramid Model of Consciousness
# (Construct #2)

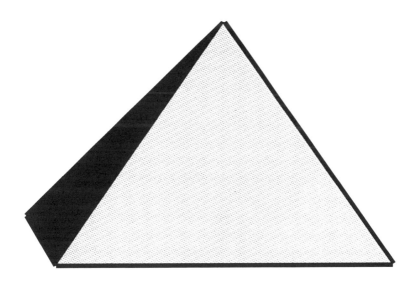

*7*he second of the four constructs for emotional skills is a new model for self-understanding: the pyramid. The pyramid is more than an ancient Egyptian tomb, or a New Age icon. Architecturally, it is the strongest and most durable structure known to man, but only if it is constructed according to certain guidelines.

The pyramid has four triangle-shaped sides, all of equal size and angle. The sides all slope toward each other, and arrive at a common point at the peak of the pyramid. When it is constructed with special regard to the relationships between the base, the height, the sides, and the angles, it can withstand the forces of nature (and man) as no other structure can. Its simplicity belies its complexity. The sheer strength of being of the pyramid offers us a metaphor for enlightenment.

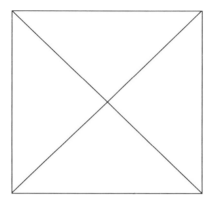

### Pyramid Model of Consciousness
### (Top View)

Each of the four sides represents an aspect of your being. One side is for the physical aspect. The second stands for the mental aspect. The third side shows us an emotional aspect. And the fourth side represents your spiritual aspect. All of us have all four aspects to our being.

Physical             Mental       Emotional        Spiritual
### Four Aspects of BEing

The triangular shape of each side of the pyramid represents skill development, peak skills being at the peak of that side. If your skills in a particular aspect were very basic, we would represent them at or near the base of that side of the pyramid. If they were well-developed skills on that side, we would show them closer to the peak. We can assess skill development on each aspect of your being against the backdrop of a central lesson to each aspect, a core lesson that exists at every level of skill on each aspect. This core lesson is the central theme of development in that aspect.

Each of us has developed some level of skill on each aspect: physical, mental, emotional, and spiritual. And most of us have one or two aspects in which our skills excel. The aspects where we excel are usually those that were modeled to us by our caretakers as we grew up. We learned the skills, of a particular aspect of being, simply by observing and mimicking those responsible for our care and nurturance when we were being raised. When we saw that something worked for someone around us, or at least it seemed to work in our naive perception, we tried it too. If it worked for us once, we used it again, practicing it until we became quite skillful in that aspect. We often refer to these as our "coping skills."

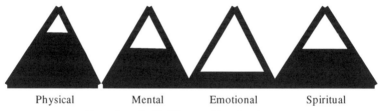

Physical          Mental          Emotional          Spiritual
## Level of Skill on Each Aspect

### The Physical Aspect

For example, you may know someone who, regardless of what it is they are experiencing, will go out and run five miles to deal with it. (You can substitute any number of verbs for "run", such as bicycle, have sex, climb, play tennis, chop wood, golf, play basketball, swim, paint, work, do aerobic exercise, dance, ride, ski, boat, surf, shoot, jump, fly, fish, fight, and so on.) And these individuals report genuinely feeling better for doing so. These are physical skills. Many people are very adept at these skills. These physical skills work to alleviate your feelings of *distress* by applying, what is called in the world of fitness, *eustress*.

One man was an avid tennis player, and a teaching pro. Anytime he felt any heightened experience, like *anger* or *frustration*, he would go out and hit several hundred tennis balls. And when he would return, he claimed to feel much better. Of course, the original experiences never disappeared. He just felt better.

Similarly, many more people today pay attention to the nutrients and chemicals they put into their bodies, knowing that what they eat has a great deal to do with what they experience. Some insist on only the cleanest air and water, the most protected sleep, the purest foods, and the most natural medicines. Breathing is a skill. Drinking is a skill. Sleeping is a skill. Eating is a skill. And healing physical ailments is a skill. These are physical skills in dealing with experiences. There is a progression of competence in each of these skills of the physical aspect.

The skill development of the physical aspect can be summarized in how well you tend to your vital force. Vital force, also known as life force, qi or chi (Chinese), ki (Japanese), or kundalini shakti (Indian) is the flow of energy through your body that distinguishes you from the dead. If a recently deceased human and a living human are lying next to each other, both bodies have exactly the same constituents. What distinguishes the living person from the dead person is their vital force.

Vital force is a very complex concept that will not be adequately defined in this presentation. It is regarded differently in different cultures. Some state that you are endowed with a finite level of vital force that you use up during your lifetime. And when your vital force is expended, so are you. Your choices are made in how efficiently you expend your vital force. Other philosophies contend that vital force can be acquired, as well as expended. And your choices are made in how deliberately you acquire, versus how well you conserve, your vital force. All of the physical skills listed above, breathing, eating, sleeping, and health skills, are the ways you go about nurturing, and perhaps acquiring, your vital force.

**The Mental Aspect**

Skills of the mental aspect have to do with how well you think: the systems of logic you use, the ability to integrate complex information into an understandable pattern. Generally speaking, these skills are more developed with education. Doctors, lawyers, nurses, teachers, engineers, scientists, and computer programmers: these are some of the people who rely largely, if not completely, on their ability to think when trying to deal with their experiences. The more education you have, the more you tend to rely on these skills. They work.

"Education" can be used in the generic sense, as well as the traditional meaning of years of school. Many people gain education through training, or through exposure; the "school of hard knocks." But whether through schooling, training or exposure, once someone feels confident that they "know" something, they tend to rely on these skills of thinking to deal with their experience. They work to relieve feelings of *distress*, at least temporarily.

The core lesson of the mental aspect of being is discipline; discipline in how your mind tracks when given specific stimuli. In every situation you are being bombarded with information through all of your senses. Your eyes see, your ears hear, and so on. Are you able to selectively screen out stimuli that are not relevant to the task you are choosing to do? And at the same time, can you maintain a complete background picture using all of the information available at that moment? Or does your mind confuse what information is needed for the task with extraneous information that could remain background? The difference is mental discipline.

The human brain can process enormous amounts of information all at the same time. For example, consider the sizable number of specific skills required to drive a car. At a minimum you must be able to enter the car, adjust your safety and comfort features such as seats, windows, safety belts, mirrors, temperature controls, and entertainment. Then you must know how to start the motor, and check instrumentation for warning signals that require attention. You need to know something about mechanics to be able to recognize different sounds the vehicle may make under different conditions. You need to know how to plan a route to arrive at your destination. You must know how to make the car go and how to make it stop safely. You have to know rules of safe driving in order to avoid unwanted impacts: distances, road signs, turns, safe mergings, and danger signals. And the list goes on and on.

Most drivers hardly give this process any thought at all, since it is so deeply integrated into their habits. But for people who decide they want to learn to drive at a later age in their lives, this can be an *overwhelming* and *terrifying* experience.

The difference is mental discipline. Those who have developed the mental discipline to focus on relevant information, and to keep in the background all other information, are able to perform the task at hand. Peak performance, in any endeavor, is the result of disciplining your mind to focus only on information that is needed for success. The central theme of all the mental skills is discipline.

## The Spiritual Aspect

The spiritual aspect involves the skills of experiencing a personal connection to the world greater than that, which is defined by our physical bodies, our minds, and our activities of daily living. In other words, how well do we get outside of ego? How well do we find a common thread between all things, people included, that unites us together? How successfully do we create a sense of purpose to our lives? These describe the skills of the spiritual aspect.

Some people are taught from a very early stage in life to pray for relief of their *distress.* So they practice the skill of praying at every opportunity. They may pray for specific physical desires, such as money, food, employment, health, etc. Or they may pray for specific feelings, such as *peace of mind, happiness, acceptance, forgiveness,* and *reassurance.* They may pray for clarity of mind, a mental endeavor. And certainly, prayer can be used to help experience greater connection to a larger reality, such as nature, unity or God. People you know may turn to their spiritual skills for any of their needs, from the very basic needs to their higher needs. This skill also works to alleviate *distress.*

On the spiritual aspect, the core lesson is faith. It is the sense of experiencing the truth of something. It defines how we see the world and the universe, how well we accept the events we do not understand. Faith defines our reason for BEing; indeed it defines our understanding of the purpose of all life. Faith is the level of connectedness we experience with the universe. As we develop our spiritual skills we progress in our level of faith.

### The Emotional Aspect

The core lesson on the emotional aspect is self-responsibility. We must learn that everything that we feel is created from within, and that neither the world, nor any specific events in it, "makes" us feel anything. In this sense then, we are the creators of every emotional experience. The sooner we learn this and claim full responsibility for our experiences, the sooner we can create our world to reflect what we truly want.

Learning the skills of self-responsibility requires emotional tools; tools which most of us have never seen before. As we learn these tools, and the skills to use them, we change our prevailing emotional experience.

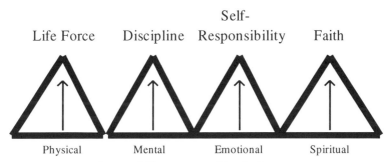

| Life Force | Discipline | Self-Responsibility | Faith |

| Physical | Mental | Emotional | Spiritual |

**Central Lesson on Each Aspect**

Level of Consciousness

If you look at the pyramid you will see that the sides slope toward each other as they rise to the peak. Imagine if those skills that you use to cope with *distress* in your life are represented on one side of the pyramid, and they rise very high. Perhaps you are very skilled in two aspects, and therefore have two sides that rise very high. But notice what happens to the architecture of the pyramid if the sides opposite these are not as high as those representing your strengths. There is no support from the opposite side to create a balance and an overall strength to the structure.

If you continue to practice only those skills that you know, then eventually you will rise high enough on that aspect to create an imbalance in your overall strength. You might even rise far enough on a single aspect that it may crumble under its own weight.

This is the essence of personal crisis. You continue to practice only those skills, which you already know, extending that aspect beyond its capacity to hold itself. When one more experience happens in which you again practice those same skills, you might suddenly find they no longer work to alleviate your *distress*. The whole aspect crumbles under its own success.

Imagine if you were a body-builder. But instead of working on both arms and both legs you decided it was enough to work only one of each ("after all, that's all you need to use most of the time.") So you pump one arm, and you work one leg, and they become very developed. Beside the visual incongruity of this picture, you would eventually realize the impracticality of such a strategy. When you tried to pick up a heavy item, the unused arm would be virtually useless, and the developed arm would undoubtedly be overstressed under the disproportionate use.

It is a silly picture, granted. But it is analogous to how we go about developing all four aspects of our being. With inadequate practice and development of some of our aspects, we become just as imbalanced as this body-builder. And we invariably end up hurting ourselves in the process.

Returning to our pyramid, imagine a horizontal plane through this pyramid. It could be the base of the pyramid, or anywhere up to and including the peak. This horizontal plane is referred to as the "Level of Consciousness." The Level of Consciousness is illustrated by a horizontal plane that is common to all four sides of the pyramid.

## Level of Consciousness

Since our Level of Consciousness must include all four aspects of BEing, then it follows that our level of consciousness is determined by our aspect of least development. For this is the only level where a horizontal plane can intersect all four aspects. For most of us, the aspect of least development is our emotional aspect. After all, it was not until the last twenty-five years or so that we began to realize that our emotions are an entirely unique part of our existence. Prior to that, we thought of them as part of our mind, our thinking capability. And we are still sometimes falling prey to this faulty model for BEing.

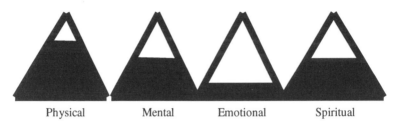

Physical          Mental          Emotional          Spiritual

## Level of Consciousness Determined by
## Aspect  of  Least  Development

No matter how developed you may be on any one of your aspects, your level of consciousness is going to be determined by your least developed aspect. You may be mentally genius, or physically prime, or spiritually holy. But if you have not learned the skills necessary to claim full responsibility for yourself, the skills of the emotional aspect, then your consciousness is going to be limited by your emotional aspect. Since most of us have never been exposed to, nor been taught, the skills of emotional development, then we definitely have limited consciousness.

Emotions! Consciousness growth requires learning about emotions for most of us, at least until our emotional development catches up to the levels of our other aspects. Then consciousness lessons will appear on whatever aspect is least developed at that time. But for now, for most of us, it is about emotions. If you are thinking to yourself that this must be applicable to others, but not you, then definitely read on. Learning how to claim your emotions is much more involved than merely "feeling *good"* or letting your emotions out. Learning how to recognize your denial of your true experience is fundamental to consciously creating what you truly want!

Remember the old model of "body, mind, and spirit?" Where does your emotional being fit in this model? Much, much too often we have been led to believe that how we felt was a result of how we thought, or of how we practiced our faith, or of our individual biochemistry. There are still many courses, books, and other specific messages that if you want to feel a certain way, you need only to learn how to think better, pray better, or put the right combination of chemicals in your body. This model is antiquated. Emotions have their own unique place in our consciousness. And it's time we all understood this.

Another feature of the pyramid is that the four sides are far apart at the base, and come closer together as they rise to the peak. When you are of low consciousness, it is difficult for you to see issues as multidimensional. That is, if something is perceived as a physical occurrence, you cannot see that it is also mental, spiritual and emotional. At a low level of consciousness, the aspects are too far separated for you to experience their relationship.

But as you rise in your level of consciousness it becomes easier for you to recognize your experience on more than one aspect. For example, what was previously experienced only on the physical aspect as a walk through the quiet forest, becomes mixed with the emotional experience of *serenity, happiness,* and *safety,* and is joined by the experience of the spiritual aspect in BEing more connected to the things around you, and is also the mental experience of acute awareness and alertness.

You can begin to see experiences as combinations of aspects. As your consciousness rises, it becomes less scattered between the four aspects, and more inclusive and more focused. Things and events in life make more sense to you. Greater understanding occurs, and *acceptance,* p*eace,* s*erenity, love, connection, unity, wisdom,* and eventually, *enlightenment.* It is for this we create our human experience.

Before you can soar, however, you must learn how to crawl, walk, and run. While most of us would like to think of ourselves as "evolved" and ready and willing to deal with enlightenment issues, it is necessary that we begin the journey from where we are; rather than from where we would like to be. You must first acknowledge the truth of where your consciousness resides, and learn the lessons being presented at that level. Enlightenment will happen as you learn to BE, here and now.

▲

## Chapter 4
## Sequence of BEing
## (Construct #3)

7he third of the four foundation constructs is called the Sequence of BEing. It is how you operate. This is the way you do things in your life, and how you arrived at the conclusion that you needed to do these things. Knowing the sequence in which you go about this process allows you to focus your energy where it can actually make a difference in your life. The first distinction you must learn to make is the difference between behavior and emotion.

### Sequence of BEing (1)

Imagine three boxes connected together in sequence, like those above. In the first box, imagine listing everything that you **do** from the time you get up in the morning to the time you go to sleep. Behavior requires doing. This would include your morning hygiene routine, choosing the clothes you wear, eating the foods you do, how you spend the time of your day in occupation or avocation or activities of daily living, the conversations you have, the words you choose, the facial expressions, the body postures, your thoughts, your choices of entertainment and of interests, and so on. The common factor among all of these activities is they all require energy from you. Even when you sleep you are frequently changing positions, and you have dreams. These, too, are doing and they require energy from you. All of these are your behaviors. Begin to see your behaviors as the expenditure of your energy.

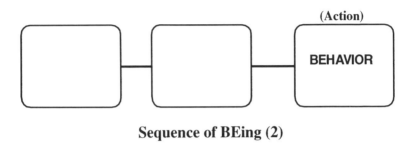

**Sequence of BEing (2)**

Considering that all behavior requires the expenditure of energy, it makes sense that this energy comes from somewhere within you. You do not do anything in your life --- eat, dress, think, converse, sleep, dream, etc. --- you do not do anything in your life unless you **feel** an emotion first!

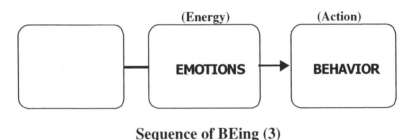

**Sequence of BEing (3)**

Emotions provide you with the energy in life that you expend in your behavior. Emotions are nothing but energy, raw energy. Furthermore, emotions are absolutely, 100% of the time, spontaneous. You do not control your emotions, and you never have. When people refer to "controlling" their emotions, they are talking about controlling what they do with their emotions, not about having or not having the emotion in the first place. You may learn to behave differently given similar experiences, but the experience is already there. While emotions are always spontaneous, they are not accidental. All emotions come from an inner source that is mostly unconscious.

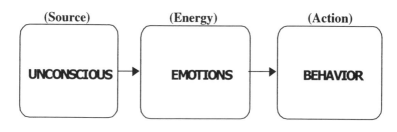

### Sequence of BEing (4)

Most of us were led to believe that other people and situations were what made us feel certain emotions: some external force. In an effort to try to control the emotions we feel, we often try to manipulate the external world. We believe that if we can get other people to behave differently, then we will feel what we want to feel.

Nowhere is this more obvious than in our language of romance. Listen to the lyrics of most love songs, regardless of style of music, and you'll hear the singer crediting their lover for their ecstasy. "You make me feel *wonderful!*" "You make me feel *whole!*" "You are the reason I'm so *happy!*" "You make me feel *loved, wanted, purposeful, natural...*"

When the relationship hits the power struggle[3], as all romantic relationships eventually will, the words change to words of blame. "You make me so *angry!*" "You make me so *sad.*" "You make me feel *unloved, unwanted, used, lonely, unattractive,* unimportant..."

When you are full flush with romance, you credit the other person for your wonderful experiences. And when you are in the pain of the power struggle, you blame the other person for your experiences. Neither of these conclusions is correct. You have been the creator of your experiences all along. All emotions are created by your beliefs, values, perceptions and early life experience, most of which exist as unconscious imprints.

Beliefs are what you have come to accept as the organization of the universe, from the infinitely small to the infinitely large. This may be based in logic, faith, mythology, traditions, superstition, education, parental messages, social mores, religion, or any number of experiences in life. Most of your beliefs were formed unconsciously.

Here is an example of a belief:  I believe we live on a planet

---

[3] Hendrix, Idem. Chapter 5

named Earth, which is the third planet from the sun in a solar system of nine planets (possibly ten and eleven are being confirmed now.) I accept that this is true even though I do not have direct experience of the validity of this belief. I think that those who claim to know about such things are credible, and they present convincing evidence. Therefore I believe it.

Another example is: I believe that there is a reflection of our own behavior in our universe. That is to say that what I get back from my universe is in some way a result of what I put into the universe. This is sometimes stated as "what goes around, comes around." Other times it is named the Law of Karma. There is no scientific evidence that supports this belief. It is one that results from my life's experience.

It is always a combination of your beliefs, values, perceptions and early life experience that create your emotional experience. No one else gets the blame, or the credit, ever!

Once you can accept this statement of cause, you might be tempted to think that it would make sense that if you want to create certain emotions in your life, then all you need to do is address your beliefs and values and perceptions and early life experience, and rearrange them so that you only feel the emotions that you desire. It may make sense, but it is not possible.

If I asked you to make a list of all your beliefs, for example, you might be able to make a very extensive list; perhaps pages and pages of them. But it would only be a list of your beliefs of which you are conscious. This is a useful exercise after you get to the stage of self-responsibility where you are seeking your lessons. However, there would be another approximately "89%" of your beliefs of which you are not conscious. It is not really possible to artificially try to manipulate these parts of you in order to create a desired set of emotions. Most of this information is not accessible, most of the time.

Your values are another part of your internal emotional source. Values are what you regard as important in your life. Some common values are honesty, integrity, truthfulness, concern for others, work ethic, family, children's welfare, individual freedom, group cooperation, lawfulness, parents' welfare, financial responsibility, independence, nationalism, community, and so on. As you can see, some values may conflict with others that you have. For instance, your concern for others may come into conflict with your value of truthfulness when someone asks you why you don't want to spend the day with them. You may be tempted to compromise truthfulness in a misguided attempt to "spare their feelings."

No two values are equivalent. Truthfulness and concern for others, while both may be of value to you, cannot be of equal value. You always have a priority order to your values, whether you are aware of that priority order or not. Much of the emotional discomfort you create in your life is a result of behaving in such a way that reflects a lower value as being more valuable than another of higher priority.

Your perceptions are yet another piece to your emotional source. Like the other pieces of emotional origin, they were mostly created through imprinting of your unconscious. Consequently, you are conscious of some of the ways in which you perceive the world, and you are unconscious of most of the ways in which you see your world.

One of the biggest assumptions about emotions relates to the area of perceptions: "The way I see the world is the way everyone else sees the world. They perceive the world the same way that I do." The fact is that each one of us sees the world differently. Every person has a unique way of perceiving the world. Your perceptions are your unique way of seeing the world. If you do not understand your particular way of perceiving the world, it is very difficult to understand the emotional experience you create from those perceptions.

An illustration of this phenomenon: Two individuals are standing on the same street corner and witness the same automobile accident. A police officer arrives at the scene and asks the witnesses for their account of the accident. Frequently, the police officer receives such varying descriptions from the witnesses that the officer might wonder if they saw the same event. One witness might report that the car that got hit was going through a stoplight, and should not have been in the intersection, and therefore it was that driver's fault.

The second witness says the ramming car was speeding to stretch a yellow light, and that was the driver who was at fault. The same events, perceived by different individuals, result in different interpretations. The events didn't change; only the perceptions were different. The police officer who interviewed the witnesses is surprised to learn that there must have been as many different accidents occurring as there were witnesses. No two reports are identical because no two people see the world in the same way. They see it the way they were trained to see it, through the "eyes" of their own perceptions.

Another demonstration can be made by trying out various good-quality sunglasses. One pair may have a blue-pink tint, and as such they call to your attention those things and events in the world that show well in that tint. But if you try out a brown-yellow tinted pair, you find that different things and events stand out to you, different features of the world around you. Different colors stand out, different buildings, different geological features. If you repeat the switch, again the world is changed. Different features and different events stand out. The foreground-background distribution changes. Both are good glasses, one pair of glasses is not better than the other. They are merely different. You experience different worlds as a result of the tint of your glasses.

Each of us has a unique "tint" to our perception that is determined by our imprinting. One person's perceptions are not better or worse than another's. But they are different. If you are trying to create *intimacy* with another person, it is necessary to learn how the other person perceives their world. It certainly behooves us in all situations to know our own tendencies in perceiving our world. What is the "tint" of your glasses?

To be fully responsible as an adult means to be aware of your experiences, to identify, update and claim your personal truth, and to make conscious decisions about your behavior. But to update your truth requires that you become conscious of what was previously unconscious. The experiences you encountered in your early developmental years had a special and permanent effect on the imprinting of your unconscious. To fully claim yourself requires that you learn as much as possible about your early life experience, and its effects upon your beliefs, your values, and your perceptions; and that you continue to update this information at every opportunity.

What was once true for you may change as you develop throughout your life. You may or may not be aware of your current and true beliefs, or values, or perceptions in any given situation. Since these parts of you were formed unconsciously, as you were imprinted, some of them may no longer be true for you, once you do become aware of them. As you do the work of consciousness you become increasingly aware of your beliefs, your values and your perceptions. As you become aware of these you will discover that some of them are true for you, and some are not. In order to learn which are true and which are not, you must learn to apply a new skill called *"The Ring of Truth."*

It is a common idiom in the American dialect to declare that an experience "rings true for me" or "doesn't ring true for me." This phrase grew out of our innate ability to resonate with messages that are true. You feel in your body when something is true or not, if you know how to listen for it. However, most of us were trained out of listening to this internal voice.

One example of this is what sometimes happens during puberty. Your nerve endings are awakening, your organism is experiencing pleasurable thoughts and emotions and body sensations. Your parents, whom you want to be pleased with you and who speak "gospel" as far as your infantile unconscious believes, tell you that sexual thoughts and sensations are wrong. So you drown out the voice of your organism, which speaks your truth, and you integrate your parents' message that these experiences are not to be believed; they are not good. Commonly, this results in sexual inhibitions. But the most detrimental development is that you become out-of-touch with the internal voice of your organism. You lose the ability to hear your truth.

Close your eyes, take a deep relaxing breath and exhale slowly. Tune into your body by excluding outside stimuli. Then speak out loud the following phrase, "My name is (use a false name)." Take another deep breath and feel how your body responds to this information. Repeat this exercise using your correct name. Notice how your body felt, in both cases, when presented with information in physical form.

When using this tool it is important to speak out loud the phrase you are testing. This employs all of the cells in your body to feel and respond. Your ears are stimulated. Your skin feels the vibrations. You use the nerves and muscles of the mouth and voice to make the sounds, and so on.

All cells in your body have the ability to feel *truth* or *non-truth*. It is an, as yet, unknown cellular device that is inherent in all living things. When your cells experience *truth* there is a *harmony* that occurs; vibrations that feel *calm*. If *non-truth* is encountered, as in the false name, your cells will respond with a *dissonance*, vibrations that *alarm*.

If you restrict your testing of this device by trying to think your way through this exercise, and do not actually allow your body to encounter the physical energy of spoken words, you will not feel the *truth*. You must say the test-phrase out loud, and then tune into your body's reaction.

Over many years of teaching this skill to hundreds of individuals, and after they have been able to get over their feelings of *silliness*, or *foolishness*, or *self-consciousness* for talking out loud to themselves, there have been common reports about the feel of *truth*. When something is experienced as true, it is commonly described as an internal sense of *calm*, a *confident* feeling, a sense of a pillar that exists through their body that *grounds* them in earth and extends out the top of their head; a resounding "Yes!" Frequently it is reported that when something is not experienced as true the individual has the feeling of *emptiness*, a *void*, a tightening or a grip in their mid-section, *butterflies* in the stomach, or they loudly hear an internal response of "No!"

*Feeling the truth* is the key to becoming more conscious. This internal *truth* has nothing to do with what you judge to be "right" or "wrong." It is not something that can be determined by anyone else but you. No parent, no spouse, no authority, no religion, no government can tell you what is *true* for you. Only you can distinguish this internal sense of truth. It is a very personal experience, a *personal truth*.

You must continuously guard against outside influence as you are first training yourself to hear what is *true* for you. Sometimes your *truth* will be unpopular. Sometimes it will mean *rejection* by others. Sometimes you may feel *alone* in the face of great opposition. You must allow none of these pressures to deter you from hearing your own *truth* as it emerges and develops. This is your *personal truth*. It is priceless in your pursuit of higher consciousness, as it becomes the power that guides you. You must regard it as the single most valuable attribute in BEing a seeker, in BEing.

As you identify your beliefs, your values, your perceptions and your early life experience in any given situation, they each must be put to the test of truth, using your *Ring of Truth*. We all carry around many beliefs, values perceptions, and even early life experiences that are not *true* for us. We usually are not aware of these untrue emotional sources, since most of them reside in our unconscious. Yet they still create certain emotional experiences, often experiences of *discomfort*. You must go further than just becoming aware your emotional sources. You must also test them, update them and *claim* them, if you are to BE fully responsible for yourself.

You cannot *claim* your emotional sources until you know whether they are *true*. As you use the *Ring of Truth* to test each source, you will encounter three possibilities: 1) the belief (or value, or perception, or early life experience) will *ring true*; 2) it will be partially *true*; 3) it will not be *true*.

If it is not *true*, then taking responsibility for yourself would require that you actively over-ride this untrue belief whenever it might appear through your emotional experience. This is done by reminding yourself, when the experience occurs, that this is not a *true* belief for you. You *re-commit* to behaving in accordance with what is *true* for you by tuning into the updated *truth* and choosing to act in accordance with it.

If the belief is partially *true*, then modification of the belief would be required before you could claim it as your personal truth. You would re-word the belief so it more nearly reflects what is true for you, and test it again. This may require multiple attempts at identifying the precise expression of your truth. Your behavior that follows should be in accordance with this updated truth, if you are to grow into higher consciousness.

If the *Ring of Truth* indicates that this emotional source is fully *true*, then claiming it as part of your essence, your *personal truth*, enables you to make conscious choices about your behavior. These skills will be described more fully in Chapter 9, "Claiming Your Personal Truth."

As you claim responsibility for your beliefs, your values, your perceptions and your early life experience, you may refer to them as your **Personal Truth**. The term *"Personal Truth"*, by definition, indicates that you have done the initial work of exploring all of the experiences of your life, up to the present moment, that are necessary in order to know your unconscious. To misuse the term is to claim a level of self-responsibility that is easily transparent. It indicates a level of growth that you will attain if you do the work, and only if you do the work. The work of psychotherapy is all about identifying your *Personal Truth*, so that you can claim it and become a responsible creator of your experience.

This is the term that goes into the third box of the Sequence of BEing, but only after most of the unconscious beliefs, values, perceptions, and early life experiences have been explored, updated, and claimed.

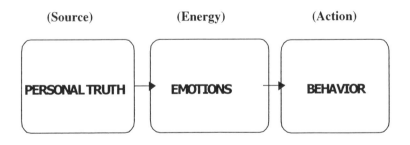

(Source)          (Energy)          (Action)

| PERSONAL TRUTH | → | EMOTIONS | → | BEHAVIOR |

### Sequence of BEing (5)

You are living your *Personal Truth* when your behavior is consistent with your *Personal Truth*. You know this is occurring when you feel the emotions of *BEing in Truth*. BEing is an experience of feeling *harmony* between your behavior, your emotions, and your *personal truth*. Consciousness is gained when, in every situation and in every moment, you can maintain a clear picture of the Sequence of BEing: What is your behavior? What is your emotion? What is your *personal truth?* Your job is to claim full responsibility for these three things, and only these three things. You will BE by living your *Personal Truth*.

▲

# Chapter 5
# Self-Responsibility
# (Construct #4)

*C*laiming full responsibility for yourself is the fourth of the foundation constructs. To be a fully responsible human you must learn to claim several different types of responsibility. This is a lifelong process of learning ever-higher skills.

First, you must know that you are 100% responsible for all of your behavior. No one makes you do anything. You are the only one in control of your body and its actions. Whatever *pressures* or *influences* you feel to act a certain way are only that: *pressures* or *influences*. Whatever reactions you might have to certain stimuli are your reactions. Whatever intent to the contrary you might have had in any given moment is moot. Your behavior is your behavior: 100% responsibility.

Second, BEing a fully responsible human means that you claim full responsibility for your emotions. You give up trying to credit, or more commonly blame, others for your emotions. All of your emotions have come from internal sources: your beliefs, your values, your perceptions and/or your early life experience. In any moment, no matter how highly *charged* it is, you are still the one who is creating your emotional experience. To be fully responsible you must learn to own all of your emotions all of the time, while you are feeling them.

Third, BEing a fully responsible human means that you cannot blame others for your emotional sources: beliefs, values, perceptions and early life experience; even those you have not yet brought into your awareness from your unconscious. Even though you may not be conscious of your emotional source, this does not relieve you of your responsibility for that source. Raising your sources to a conscious level when the moment arises, putting them to the test of the truth and then *claiming your responsibility for your truth*, is what the real work of consciousness is all about. This is a lifelong process for most people, since so much of the source of our emotions is unconscious.

Learning to separate your behavior from your emotions from your personal truth, and claiming full responsibility for all three is what begins to develop your consciousness. So finish the picture of the Sequence of BEing by enclosing the three boxes in another box.

**100% Self-Responsibility**

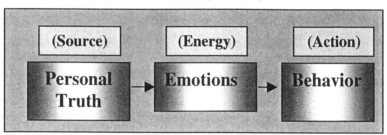

**Sequence of BEing (6)**

This illustrates the work you must do to claim conscious control of your life. You must learn to claim full responsibility for all of your behavior, all of your emotions, and your personal truth. This constitutes 100% of your responsibility.

This issue of "self-responsibility" is the central lesson on the emotional aspect. It is the single most important issue in advancing on your emotional aspect, and thus the attainment of higher levels of consciousness. Claiming 100% self-responsibility is full-time work.

"Responsibility" is a word that *grates uncomfortably* on many individuals. You might be one who hears a critical parent, pointing and wagging a finger at you, saying, "This wouldn't have happened if you had been more responsible!" Or, "When are you going to grow up and be responsible?" It often is perceived as a list of "shoulds" coming from some authority figure. It may be helpful to break the word apart and think of it as "response ability", or the ability to respond.

What you are striving for as you claim your personal truth and your emotions is to be able to consciously choose behavior that is consistent with your Personal Truth. Most people, as they become aware of an event or a situation, feel their emotions and then do some behavior; feel and do, feel and do. They have no idea that they even have a personal truth, let alone claim it. They probably were not even aware of their emotions, before taking some course of action. The real sources of their emotion remain hidden to them. They believe that emotions are created from sources outside of them. This connection, between feeling and doing, is referred to as a reaction, and is entirely unconscious. Consciousness begins to come when your reactions are minimized, or eliminated altogether.

100% Self-Responsibility

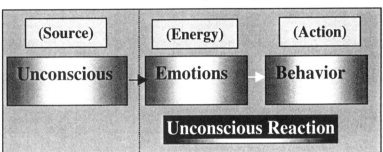

## Sequence of BEing (7)

Behavior that is chosen consciously is called a response. You become aware of an event or situation in the world by feeling your emotions. By claiming responsibility for your emotions, you explore them and their sources. This brings to light the beliefs, values, perceptions, or early life experience that need to be reviewed, updated as necessary and claimed. By claiming your Personal Truth, you harness the energy in those emotions. Then and only then are you able to direct that energy into behavior that reflects your truth. You have responded to your world in a conscious manner. You feel, claim your Personal Truth, and choose truthful behavior.

By putting this loop, to seek consciousness, into the Sequence of BEing, you will be responding to the world instead of reacting to it. Another way of saying this is you will be increasing your ability to respond to the world; your "response ability." This picture puts "responsibility" into perspective. It is not just another list of "shoulds" or another way of debasing yourself. It is the ability to be conscious at all times, and thereby respond to the world.

**100% Self-Responsibility**

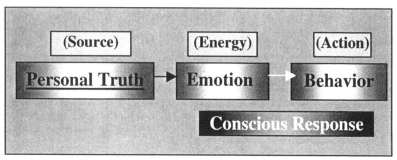

**Sequence of BEing (8)**

Self-responsibility is a two-sided lesson. On one side is the on-going lesson of learning to claim more of the responsibility that is yours. On the other side is learning how to reject the responsibility that is not yours. Just as you are responsible for all of your behavior, all of your emotions, and all of your Personal Truth, you are not responsible for any one else's behavior, anyone else's emotions, or anyone else's sources of emotion. There can only be a total of 100% responsibility. The degree, to which you accept responsibility for someone else's behavior, emotions, or sources, is the same degree to which you are failing to claim the responsibility that is yours.

Learning to refuse all responsibility for the behavior, emotions, or personal truth of anyone else but you, is every bit as challenging as learning to claim what is yours. If you attempt to take any responsibility for someone else's behavior (as in, you made them do something), or for their emotions (you made them feel something), or for their personal truth (you made them believe something or choose a particular value), then you cannot be claiming 100% of your responsibility. You cannot take responsibility for anyone else and still fulfill your responsibility. Any time you try to do this you are missing the opportunity for you to practice consciousness.

Similarly, coercing someone to behave in a certain way does not make you responsible for his or her behavior. They still have full responsibility over the actions that they chose to do, whether they claim that responsibility or not. (You would be responsible, however, for your coercive behaviors.)

Inviting an emotional experience in someone, by predicting their reaction to a certain behavior, does not make you responsible for his or her emotions. Your behavior is merely an invitation to feel, which they will react to emotionally in their unique way, according to their unique imprinting. When you smile at someone you are perhaps inviting him or her to feel *acceptable*, *welcomed*, *appreciated*, and *warm*. Many people would react to this behavior with these emotions. However, many other people would react to your invitation with *suspicion*, *alarm*, *fear*, and *rejection*. Since your behavior, of any kind, can elicit such varied reactions, it is easily understandable how you cannot claim responsibility for their emotional reaction. Your behavior can invite emotions. It cannot cause them.

Whenever you attempt to take responsibility that belongs to someone else, or you refuse to claim responsibility that belongs to you, you will create problems between you and that other person. In relationships of all kinds, nothing is more important than staying clear about who is responsible for what behavior, who is responsible for what emotions, and who is responsible for the beliefs, values, perceptions and early life experience that were the source for those emotions. As you will see later, all relationship problems are due to confusion over who is responsible for what!

> *All relationship problems are due to confusion over who is responsible for what.*

There is no other issue that causes emotional *dismay* such as confusion over responsibility. Self-responsibility, with its two sides, will be a recurrent lesson in the pursuit of higher consciousness. It is one you will need to learn at ever-deeper levels. Commit to the goal of claiming 100% of your self-responsibility. It is the vehicle that takes you into higher consciousness.

▲

# PART   II:  The Path of Emotion

## Chapter 6
## Your Emotions as an Internal Guidance System

*7*he four foundation constructs necessary for learning the skills to claim higher levels of consciousness are: The Unconscious; The Pyramid Model of Consciousness; The Sequence of BEing, and 100% Self-Responsibility. If you understand these constructs you are ready to learn the skills needed for emotional development. Your emotions are an internal guidance system that leads you on a path of constant development in consciousness, when you know how to use them.

To use your emotions effectively as a tool for enlightenment you need to understand how your emotions were first trained. Recall from the first construct, the unconscious, that when you first entered this world you were nothing but unconscious. Remember that the sole purpose of your unconscious is to guarantee your survival, which was contingent upon the good will of your caretakers. Your unconscious was the device for training your emotions so that your survival would be enhanced.

All infants have emotions, including you. Your emotions were created from your internal sources, your beliefs, your values, your perceptions and your experience (all of which was early life at that time), as explained in the third construct, The Sequence of BEing. Since you had no consciousness then, you had no means for testing any of these sources for their validity, their truth. If you were hungry or cold or injured, you felt emotional *discomfort*. If you needed company, you felt the emotion of *loneliness* or *desire for intimacy*. If you were scolded you might have experienced an emotion of *rejection* or *fear*. You had emotions, and you felt them, as all infants do. And you acted out that energy with the behaviors of an infant.

From the very first day of your life your caretakers, usually your parents, were giving you messages about the acceptability of your behavior that resulted from your emotions. Your parents might have given you extra attention when you cooed, giggled, and smiled. You, in your infantile unconscious state, quickly learned that these emotions were *acceptable*, even *desirable*. They were life-enhancing emotions, since they helped to guarantee your survival.

However, if you learned that whining, crying, and screaming brought you no attention; or even worse, these behaviors brought you the wrath of your parents; then you quickly learned to associate the emotions that preceded these behaviors as *unacceptable,* even life threatening.

In this manner, in a relatively short time, you learned that all of your emotions fell into one of two categories to varying degrees: *acceptable* or *unacceptable.* All of your emotions were identified as either life enhancing, acceptable, or life threatening, unacceptable.

Today, you unconsciously continue with these same definitions of your emotions that you learned while a child. You probably refer to the categories of your emotions as either positive emotion or negative emotion. As a child you learned that certain emotions were *acceptable* and therefore life enhancing. These you regard as positive. The emotions you learned as being *unacceptable* are those you regard as negative.

Emotions are neither positive nor negative. Only your early life experiences defined them this way. The only difference between positive emotions and negative emotions is that you were trained to believe that some of them enhanced your survival while others threatened your survival. The difference between positive emotions and negative emotions is a direct result of the level of acceptability for the emotion expressed to you by your caretakers at the time when you experienced it as a child. Positive emotions are those that met with acceptance, and therefore helped to guarantee your survival. Negative emotions are those that were met with unacceptance, and therefore threatened your survival.

One common misconception about emotions is that your definitions about which emotions are positive and which are negative are the same as everyone else's. The opposite proves true. If you were an infant that received extra attention and nurturance when you were feeling emotions of *sadness* or *anger*, then you probably learned to regard these emotions as positive. These emotions were given *acceptance* by your caretakers. Yet another infant who experienced similar emotions of *sadness* or *anger* may have been left alone, and not attended to nor nurtured. That infant found *unacceptance* in that environment and learned to regard these emotions as life threatening, negative. As adults these two people would have different regard for their emotions of *sadness* or *anger*. One would regard them as positive. The other adult would regard them as negative. In reality, it is neither. It is your unique set of definitions that color an experience as positive or negative.

To be able to use your emotions effectively to guide you toward enlightenment, you will learn to regard all of your emotions as neither positive nor negative, but merely as another experience from which you can draw energy. Judging your emotions as either "good" or "bad," invites you then to attempt to manipulate your emotions, making it impossible to follow your Path of Emotions. "Good" emotions are received as one of life's pleasures to be enjoyed. And "bad" emotions are resisted as one's of life's tribulations. But if you learn to experience your emotions without judging them as positive or negative, then you can take full advantage of following the path they are presenting, which leads you to your personal truth, to truthful behavior and toward higher consciousness and enlightenment. You will be feeling your way along!

Since emotions are nothing but raw energy, it is helpful to picture how your unique definitions of positive and negative emotions have been affecting you. To illustrate these states of energy we can use an imaginary oscilloscope. This is an electronic device that is used to measure electrical activity. An oscilloscope is used to show human heart rhythms. This is the instrument that shows the heartbeat, or none when the patient's heart stops beating. Oscilloscopes can be used to measure all forms of electrical energy. Since emotions are energy, we are going to create an oscilloscope to demonstrate this energy.

Here is a typical, round screened oscilloscope. We have a baseline drawn horizontally through the middle of the screen. All the area above the baseline we will label positive. And all the area below the baseline we will label negative.

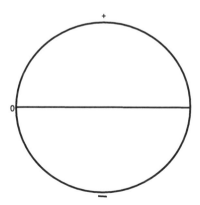

**Oscilloscope**

Infants come into this world with the ability to fully feel all of their experience. Anyone who has been around infants has witnessed their ability to display *joy* and *bliss* in one moment, *discomfort* the next moment, *curiosity*, *pleasure*, *rage*, *fear*, *comfort*, and *satisfaction*, all within minutes. Infants are completely fluid in their emotional experience, without internal judgment or *desire* to manipulate.

Let's illustrate what your emotional energy looked like when you were an infant. Notice the full and equal curves in both the positive phase and the negative phase of energy. In mathematics, this would be known as a sine curve.

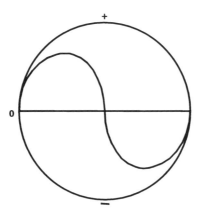

**Emotional energy at birth**

Your unconscious determined your subsequent lessons. As your unconscious associated survivability with each experience, due to the acceptability of your outward behavior as defined by your caretakers, your unconscious had to develop a means for eliminating those experiences that threatened your survival. Your unconscious began to exercise an inherent survival skill known as "denial."

Since certain experiences were *unacceptable* to your parents, you learned that in order to survive (or so your unconscious led you to believe), you needed to extinguish these experiences. You needed to make sure they did not occur, or if they did, you needed to keep them from showing in your behavior.

You can never get rid of experience, what you feel is what you feel. Your experience is not subject to your decision-making. Instead, you learned to bury these experiences inside your unconscious, so that they ceased to threaten your survival. Your unconscious put these experiences in a kind of organic recycle bin. You did not get rid of them, but they were deleted from your awareness. As far as you were concerned they were eliminated. You no longer had any awareness of or connection to these emotions. You either diminished the intensity of these experiences, or deleted them from your awareness. You did not feel them. In reality, they continued. But you could not afford the luxury of acknowledging them.[4]

For example, recall when you were learning to ride a tricycle at age 3 or 4. You might have made a turn too sharply and toppled over, skinning your knee as a result. You ran inside with the droplets of blood marking your way to your mom's side. You felt the need for her to *comfort* you through your *fear* and *discomfort*, your brush with death in your eyes. Instead, she said to you, "Toughen up and stop that crying! It's only a scratch and nothing to be *upset* about. Now, go outside and play."

Your unconscious translation of this experience may have been, "Mom is not *pleased* with me when I show *fear* and need for *nurturance*. So, I'd better not allow myself those feelings." The more this translation is reinforced, the more convinced (i.e. imprinted) your unconscious becomes. The next time you trip down the icy stairs, you pick yourself up, swallow down your *fright* and quickly wipe away your tears before your mom looks out the window to see you.

This is the essence of denial. The life threatening experiences have occurred. Your unconscious has associated unacceptability with them. They are real and they exist. They are stored forever in the unconscious. But you lose awareness of them. They hide themselves deep within your unconscious, for they are a threat to your very survival, nothing less.

---

[4] Consciousness and awareness are not entirely accurate terms at this stage of development. Awareness is a term used to describe when one notices something and retains long-term memory of it. Consciousness, the differentiated "self", comes around age six. At this stage of infancy and into early childhood, it would be more correct to use the term "sub-conscious" or "pre-conscious." The authors chose to not introduce another level of complexity here.

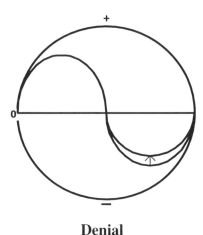

## Denial

Denial affects the energy of these emotions. By hiding this experience from your awareness, you no longer have it available for your use. You diminish its intensity. Instead of the natural, fluid emotional curve, that is every person's birthright, you now lower the energy level.

Denial is the first and most universal emotional skill. Everyone has this skill. Everyone employs it, to varying degrees. It is the emotional skill inherent in your unconscious for the purpose of survival. Denial is an essential skill, and it is one that remains useful. You can successfully diminish the intensity of life threatening experiences, by employing the skill of denial. When life is truly threatened, this skill is extremely valuable.

In an emergency you would not want the people helping you to be tuning into their *discomfort* or *fear* or *sadness*. This would interfere with their ability to perform the procedures they have been trained to do. If someone you *loved* were about to be injured by an on-coming automobile, you wouldn't want to cripple your ability to react because you were tuning into your *fear*. Soldiers in battle could not very effectively perform the jobs they have been trained for, and that governments ask them to do, if they become *overwhelmed* in their experiences of the moment.

Denial is an appropriate skill to use in a situation where physical health or safety is an emergency. Immediate survival is best left to the reactions of the unconscious. (Remember that unconscious does not mean nor imply "unthinking." It merely refers to the state of unawareness of true motivation and true experience. Thinking occurs on a different aspect of BEing altogether, the Mental Aspect.)

Denial, then, is not necessarily a problem. Denial is a survival skill, one that serves humans very well in times when immediate survival is the highest need. The problem with denial is not in having this skill available to use when necessary and appropriate Denial becomes a problem when it is over-used, in all other situations other than those involving immediate survival.

You discovered early that denial worked to get rid of unwanted experiences, or so it seemed since the experiences were lost to awareness. In the absence of emotional training, where you would be introduced to other emotional skills, you would most likely attempt to use denial to get rid of all experiences with a negative label. You practiced what you knew and what seemed to work. And you practiced and practiced and practiced.

All the time you were reducing the intensity of your negative experiences, not by making the experiences go away, but by diminishing your awareness of them. Now your energy graph might look something like this, with the diminishing intensity of your negative emotions:

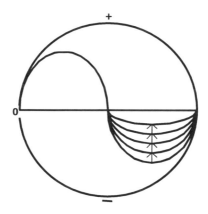

**Denial of negative emotions**

Like the physical law, there is an emotional law that you cannot reduce one state of energy without reducing the reciprocal state of energy. One of the emotional events that has been occurring throughout your life is that, as you practiced your skill of denial in an attempt to reduce the intensity of your negative experiences, you had a similar reduction of intensity of your positive emotions.

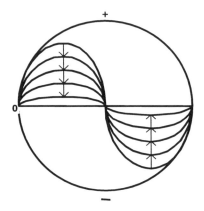

**Effect of denial on positive emotions**

The total sum of energy available remains equally divided between the positive phase and the negative phase. Our oscilloscope would read the energy distribution like this:

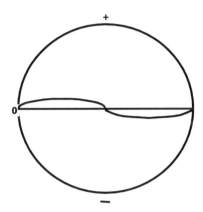

## Emotional energy diminished due to denial

This probably felt like a fair trade, as you were young and maturing. It seemed okay to loose some of that "youthful *enthusiasm*" if it meant losing those intense negative emotions. But by continuing to practice denial all of your adult life, you have continued to lose more of the intense feelings that were *desirable*. You cannot diminish one state of emotion without also diminishing the reciprocal state.

In studying aging, and the experiences of the elderly, the most common experience described is *depression*. While becoming old is often referred to as the stage of *loss*, since there are the common losses of physical abilities, productive work, and close relationships, the *depression* referred to is not that associated with these losses. These losses are a generally accepted part of growing old. Instead, the *depression* associated with aging is the *depression of apathy*.

*Apathy* is the feeling of "*really not caring*." The flowers aren't as colorful as they used to be. The sky isn't as blue as you remembered it. The music isn't as *pleasant*. The relationships really don't *matter* much. Life isn't as *good* as it used to be. *Depression of apathy* is the result of a lifetime of practicing denial to reduce the intensity of the negative emotions, all the while unknowingly reducing the intensity of the positive emotions too. The energy curve at this point in life looks like this:

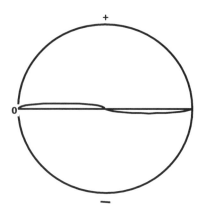

## Emotional energy after a lifetime of denial

Also true in emotional laws, as in physical laws, "a flatline is a flatline is a flatline." When the energy runs out, there is no more life. It may seem more than a little ironic that the very skill your unconscious developed to assure survival is also the one that will ultimately lead you to your death. Denial is the systematic elimination of the very energy necessary for BEing.

Most people, upon examining this situation, would respond by saying they will work to maximize their positive experiences. They will take as much of those as they can get. There are many books and courses that lead you to believe that you can do this. They try to tell you that if you think more positively then you can create more positive experience. Or if you practice affirmations of a positive nature, then you can create more positive experience. Or if you smile more....    Or if you pray sincerely....    Or if you meditate consistently...

The problem is not defined by our lack of positive experience. Most of us would *welcome* all of the positive experience we could get. The problem is not in the positive end of the graph. The problem of lost emotional energy leading to *apathy* and *depression* is due to the overuse of this first and universal emotional skill: denial. And that occurs in the negative end of the graph. It is here you must focus your attention, first and forever.

▲

## Chapter 7
## Willingness

Self-destruction is the natural conclusion of a life spent in denial. This single emotional skill will keep you safe in the moment, at the cost of your long-term interests. If, for example, while hunting for your food, you encounter a bear, denial will make it possible for you to flee from danger. While running from an immediate danger keeps you safe, it also keeps you from eating. The skill that saves you from one problem is also the skill that creates a more pervasive problem.

Safety is, undoubtedly, a top priority in some moments. But it cannot remain the top priority in all moments. If you keep it as such, you will never accomplish any other goals. The need for safety must be viewed skeptically if you are to ever chance the risk necessary to encounter the world. The only purpose of the unconscious is to assure your safety. If you allow your unconscious to reign over your consciousness, then you will probably always be safe. But you will also be working toward your own demise.

Claiming consciousness, which includes hearing and attending to your unconscious, is the only way to establish a standard by which you can adequately assess potential risks and your willingness to deal with those risks. By deciding to be consciously in charge of your own life, you are choosing to not allow your unconscious to run you from "behind the scenes."

The unconscious, with its one emotional skill of denial, runs continuously, in every moment, in every situation. If you are ready to claim control of your life, you must learn and establish a pathway of consciousness to override your unconscious. This pathway requires emotional awareness. Denial is an unconscious emotional skill that diminishes your awareness of your emotions. Denial is an unwillingness, that occurs unconsciously, to be aware of what is really happening within your emotional realm.

The pathway into consciousness always begins with consciously choosing to be willing to feel all the emotions that you feel, and choosing to be willing to deal with them. Willingness overrides the unconscious pattern of diminishing awareness of your emotions. Willingness is what reverses the energy graph. Instead of reducing your awareness of your emotional energy, you will begin to increase your awareness of the energy available to you. Willingness is the first of the four steps to the Path of Emotion, the internal guidance system that allows you to claim higher levels of consciousness.

The pattern of the emotional energy that you were born with still exists within you. You never really lost the energy. You have only lost your awareness of it, and therefore wasted it. It is your birthright to be able to feel the full spectrum of human emotions. Awareness is what restores the availability of this energy. And it is willingness that begins the process of awareness. Willingness is the first act of consciousness. It is a choice. To consciously choose to be willing to feel and to deal; this is the first of the emotional skills that can open the door to enlightenment. Willingness.

As you choose willingness, you will be reclaiming the energy that is available to you through your emotions. Your negative emotion curve will increase in intensity. And your positive emotion curve will follow. This is how to truly create greater positive experience in your life: be willing to have greater experience, regardless of how it is defined. Here is a graphic picture on our oscilloscope of what a healthy energy curve will look like:

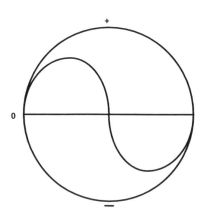

**Healthy emotional energy**

In another philosophy, this depiction of energy might have been drawn like this, to show the natural ebb and flow of all energy and its resulting balance in the whole:

## Phases of energy as symbolized in the sign of the Tao

The four constructs, described in Part I, provide a foundation. Using your emotions to guide you to ever-deeper self-awareness is the key to creating a reality that is more consistent with your truth. In order to use your emotions, you must first make a conscious decision to make yourself available to this information. This is the decision to be willing to feel all of your emotional experience. This is the first act of consciousness: choose to be willing to feel all that you feel and to deal with all that you feel.

Willingness is the first of a four-step method for using your emotions to gain higher consciousness. Willingness is what overrides the one emotional skill you have been practicing all of your life, denial. When your unconscious is warning you not to feel certain experience, you need to talk yourself through the *fear* or *hesitancy*. At these times, you will be challenged to re-affirm your choice to be willing to feel and to deal. Willingness cannot be an intermittent choice. Your commitment to your pursuit of higher consciousness must be complete.

You cannot dabble in consciousness, and expect to realize higher levels. You cannot choose to be willing some of the time, when it is convenient, or when it doesn't interfere with the other things you want to do, or when you determine that the moment is safe enough. If you leave any opportunity for your unconscious to reclaim its purpose, to assure your safety, it will do so with every emotion that you define as negative.

You must choose to be willing to feel and deal with all of your emotions, especially those that are defined as negative by you. It does not mean you need to arbitrarily create negative experiences, so that you can practice willingness. It usually does not mean you will immediately fall into *depression, chaos,* or *crisis.* But the prospect of having to actually feel those emotions that you have been actively denying often does cause some *apprehension* and *anxiety.*

This is understandable if you imagine this process from the point of view of your unconscious. For years it has been doing its job of removing your awareness of your negative emotions in an honest effort for survival. Now you come along and willingly allow awareness of these emotions. Your unconscious is going to warn you of the dangers of such actions. "Alert! Alert! Don't go in there! It will kill you!" "Danger, danger, danger! Do not go any closer!" It thinks it is protecting your best interests by keeping your awareness limited and diminished. You can count on many such warnings coming in the form of *uncomfortable* emotions, some perhaps as strong as *unexplained terror* or *self-doubt* and *confusion.*

If you are a parent, you might imagine how you would react if your child was in grave danger. Most *loving* parents would *willingly* sacrifice their own life, if it meant saving the life of their child. It's not that they want to lose their own life. It's just that their *love* for their child is so deep that they remain constantly vigilant to any danger that might harm the child. It is a *duty* they feel. It is not *heroic.* It is not *desirable.* It is felt to be the *natural order* of things. In fact, any parent who has survived the death of their child is left with the *unnaturalness* of this as one of their ongoing issues. In terms of life stressors, this is considered to be catastrophic, requiring years of professional assistance to adequately integrate.

Your unconscious is very much like this ever-vigilant parent who will sacrifice its own life in order to preserve yours. It is through total focus on survival that this part of us tries to steer us away from perceived danger through very loud internal warnings. The unconscious is not an enemy to be overthrown. It is a totally committed part of yourself that needs to be *attended to, respected,* and dealt with, in *kindness* and *appreciation.* To practice willingness to feel, you need to do some self-talk at the point of emotional distress. Self-talk gets you through the inherent resistance. First, remember that no emotion can kill you, despite what your unconscious may be screaming to the contrary. There are recorded exceptions to this rule, such as being *frightened* to death, or *stressed* into heart failure, and so on. But these exceptions are very rare, and they usually involve years of denial of an emotion that becomes overwhelming. It is not the choice to be willing that creates the danger, but the attempts to continue in denial!

Make an ally of your unconscious. It has been working 24-hours a day, all your life, to safeguard your survival. The skill of denial will periodically have use in your life. You are trying to expand your repertoire of emotional skills, not eliminate any, including denial. The problem with denial is in its overuse, not its availability in your bag of tools. Don't try to fight your unconscious. Acknowledge its purpose and its efforts, and then commit fully to consciously choosing to be willing to feel all that you feel in each moment, and then to deal with what you feel using the new skills you are learning. Denial is a life-saving skill, only to be used in case of a physical emergency that threatens your life or that of someone around you. Usually, blood will be flowing before denial is a useful skill; life and death situations, where the physical safety of you or someone you care about is truly the highest priority.

You cannot afford to allow yourself to use denial in any non-emergency situation. If you try to rationalize to yourself that denial is necessary or okay right now, that you will get back to this experience later, then you will be turning down the intensity of your experience in all situations. Denial is indiscriminate. Use it here, and it spreads everywhere. Denial is insidious. Beware the costs for allowing it freedom in your experience. It will slow your growth, and maybe even stop it. It will prevent you from BEing fully present in any situation. There is always a cost to using denial, even in life threatening situations. If denial is ever used, in order to prevent loss of life or ability, then the experience must be fully processed as soon as possible afterward. If denial was necessary and prevailed over an extended period of time, such as in combat, then much effort, and professional assistance, is needed to review, process, and integrate those experiences.

Choosing to be willing to feel all experience is not just a single, one-time choice. It is not even a choice to be made periodically. It requires an on-going commitment to remain open to your experience, regardless of convenience, *comfort*, or subsequent emotion. The choice needs to be made again and again as new *discomforts* arise, anytime you feel an emotion that is labeled negative in your set of definitions. You must watch for denial sneaking in and taking up charge where it used to have it. You need to check your level of denial in every situation. Check in with yourself regularly to watch for denial that may have re-emerged without your noticing it. You have created hundreds of ways to exercise denial over the years. Learn to see your ways. Check your denial! "What do I feel now? What do I feel now, in this moment? What about now? And this moment?"

Here is an example of how denial is insidious, and leads to vague or unexplainable *discomfort*, *unhappiness*, and *malaise*. A 28-year-old woman was referred by her physician to psychotherapy for complaints of *anxiety*. She had heart palpitations, difficulty sleeping, and recurring *fears* of contracting cancer.

During her initial interview she was unable to identify any current or recent significant problems. She reported that she and her husband had jobs that were enjoyable and secure. They were *enjoying* their marriage and their 9-month old baby. She felt genuinely *perplexed* about her episodes of *anxiety*. She also reported that she felt it necessary to leave for work earlier and earlier, as she was "*swamped*" there. This put her son in the care of her husband more and more each week.

When talking about her baby she seemed to idealize her experiences with him since his birth: no problems, no feelings of being *overwhelmed*, no *fears*, and so on. She presented a picture that this was the perfect child and the perfect mother-child relationship. Questions regarding this ideal presentation were met with a reaction of *discomfort* and *nervousness*. She eventually became *annoyed* that "so much time was being wasted in this area" where she felt everything was so "*right*."

As she continued to feel these emotions, it became clear to her that she did indeed have *discomfort* in the area of her child that she had been in denial about. She tuned into her *fear* of taking on the *awesome responsibility* for her new son's caretaking. She realized that this *responsibility* meant the difference between his survival and death. She also realized that she was *surrendering* this *responsibility* to her husband each time she left the baby in his care, as she went off to work.

It became clear to her that her *anxiety* was the result of the *conflict* she was experiencing about *responsibility* for her child: she *wanted* the child, she didn't want to be so completely responsible for him;

she felt *responsible* for him, but she was *surrendering* this responsibility as she went to work. She felt this and then that, and later that and then this. Her emotions were telling her she needed to confront and deal with this internal *conflict*. And they spoke a language that eventually broke through her denial and got her attention through *unexplainable anxiety*.

Some of the other ways in which denial might be exhibited:

- Addictions (alcohol, recreational drugs, prescription medications, gambling, excessive work, excessive sex, food, etc.);
- Development of physical symptoms (stress-exacerbated ulcers, high blood pressure, heart attack, failing vision, cancers, obesity, eating disorders, crippling "accidents")
- Overuse of humor (attempting to "keep things light")
- Minimizing experience ("we hardly have any conflicts," "we never fight,")
- Positive thinking
- Convincing others that everything is fine
- Blaming others, misplacing responsibility ("If only he would change everything would be alright.")
- "We just need some communication skills."
- Relationship partners continually rescuing each other (ensure each other's safety by each of your denial)
- Invalidating self-talk ("toughen-up, quit whining, grow up")
- Criticizing others; invalidating others to protect your own denial system ("You're being too sensitive, too analytical, too intense, etc.")
- Using any of the other three aspects to reduce or eliminate discomfort ("Surrender to Jesus;" extra hard physical work; seeking out a mental challenge)
- Idealizing parents; Idolizing parents; Hero-worship of any kind
- Using "if only..." thoughts and phrases ("If only we could have another baby." "If only he didn't have to travel so much.")

This is not to say that any time you see these behaviors they are necessarily reflecting denial from that person. But these are common enough examples of expressions of denial that it is useful to suspect denial whenever you see them.

> *"Fraud and falsehood only, dread examination.*
> *Truth invites it."*
>
> (Thomas Cooper)

Denial frequently escalates into *defensiveness* and power struggles in relationships that are important to you. Denial can even escalate further into *revenge*, feuding and war. Denial is at the root of all injury and pain, all power struggles and separation, all misunderstanding and conflict, all *hatred* and *intolerance*, all inhumanity. Denial is the root of all *discomfort* and *dissension*. Indeed, denial is the root of all *evil*.

Denial is always harmful. Any level of denial is harmful. Even the denial employed for the immediate care of a person with a life threatening injury, which may be the only time denial is justifiable, is harmful. Nothing truthful needs the protection of denial, and nothing truthful benefits from denial. The more you protect your denial, the more harmful it becomes. Each time you exercise your denial you give unconscious support and validation to the cause of all harmful unconscious behavior.

Check your denial! Always! Choose to be willing to feel what you feel. This will begin a process of creating more conscious behavior.

▲

## Chapter 8
## Exploration

*I*magine if you were put into a large, dark room, depriving you of your sense of sight. You would want to explore your surroundings, enough to know if there even existed a source of light. You would have to feel around in the dark by touching things, and attempting to recognize them, without use of your vision.

If you were in this room long enough, you would eventually come to recognize some of the items that shared your space, simply by touch. You would eventually master the environment, if you continued to feel around in the dark. In so doing you might even discover the existence of a light source, perhaps even a light switch that would then illuminate your surroundings and allow you greater mobility and freedom.

By using your emotions to encounter the world, you have the opportunity to familiarize yourself with your world in a new way. You might even discover the existence of a light source, perhaps even a light switch that would illuminate your whole world, allowing you unlimited freedom.

Another word for emotions is "feelings." Indeed, emotions give a new way of sensing your world. They allow you to "feel" your world, to "feel" your way along. But you can only feel your world if you make yourself available to your feelings. Check your denial. Choose willingness to feel all of your experiences.

> *"Ask and you shall receive; knock and the door shall be opened; seek and you shall find. "*
> (Jesus of Nazareth, reported by Matthew)

The second step of the Path of Emotion is to thoroughly explore the experiences you are now willing to feel. Exploration is an exercise in discovery. It cannot be hurried. Exploration requires becoming familiar with the territory. This is when you want to get to know what the experience feels like, from all different perspectives. Look for the distinguishing characteristics of this experience from all others.

## Perceptions

Before beginning your exploration, however, it is helpful and wise to question what it is that you are observing or perceiving in the world that invites you to feel what you feel. You may or may not be perceiving correctly. Questioning and clarifying your perceptions assures you that you will be dealing with emotions that are relevant to real stimuli, rather than imaginings. Are you perceiving what you think you are perceiving? Are you only perceiving part of the picture, or misperceiving altogether? Checking out your perceptions means questioning the validity of every stimulus, whether it is physical (i.e. visual, auditory, tactile, olfactory, gustatory), or whether it is mental (i.e. ideas, understanding), or emotional (i.e. feelings, intuition), or spiritual (i.e. connections, faith).

Since all of us have a unique "tint" to our perceptions, you know you will perceive things and events in your own unique way. You may hear certain words as threatening or personalized. You may understand certain actions as "for" you or "against" you. You may make initial judgments about experiences that will change as you replay those experiences in your mind. It is very helpful to continuously expand your awareness of your own perceptions, so you can fully appreciate, and therefore anticipate, the tint you put on experiences. Checking out your perceptions means taking specific steps to discover how you tinted an event to create the emotional experience in a certain way.

If you had been in a business meeting in which you experienced feeling *unheard, angry, disappointed* and *discouraged*, you could go to the person whom you felt offended by, and check out your perception. "Bill, it seemed to me that you did not hear me in our meeting when I made a proposal. I want to check out whether you didn't hear me, or if you were ignoring me."

If Bill responds by saying, honestly, that he did not hear your proposal, and if he had heard you he would have certainly given it due consideration, and you perceive Bill as being honest and sincere, then your experience of that event will probably be different than it was originally. Your emotions would be much less *distressful*. The only change is a different perception of the same events, which was made possible by the relatively simple act of checking out your original perception.

Your inquiry of the accuracy of your perceptions must begin from a place of *humility*, the *humility* of knowing you may not be right, no matter how sure you think you are. It is entirely possible that you completely misperceive any given event. And in so doing, you have created an entire experience that has no foundation in reality. In approaching every situation with this *humility*, you are far more likely to gain full cooperation from other people as you pursue your enlightenment. Their cooperation can be very helpful in your effort to clarify your perceptions. The other person is much more likely to answer you with complete honesty and *sincerity* if they are not trying to defend themselves against an attack by you.

If you approach them with a sense of righteousness, a belief that you are right before having all the information, you will usually invite *defensiveness* in the other person, and have much greater difficulty in communicating about your perception. Exercising *humility* does not mean you must *discredit* your perception, either. Your perception is your perception, based on the information up to that moment. It may be entirely accurate, or it may be skewed in any number of ways. Own your perception for what it is: the beginning of an experience. It helps to remember that, even if you did perceive correctly, the other person did not create your emotion. You create every emotion, from internal sources, regardless of the events of the outside world.

You can check out your perceptions in any situation by asking questions in regard to them. If you are interacting with another human, *wondering* aloud if you are perceiving accurately can help avoid many conflicts. "I perceive you as saying..." "Am I hearing you accurately?" "I wonder if you mean to be saying..."

While you will often phrase questions with an "am I right..." kind of format, being "right" is not what you are after. For being right usually means someone else must therefore be wrong. Playing the "who's right and who's wrong" game is a dynamic that usually leads to a power struggle. Right and wrong discussions are not very helpful in the process of claiming self-responsibility. What you are striving for is accuracy and clarity, not "being right."

If you are not interacting with another human, you can check out your perception in any situation by asking yourself if you might be misperceiving or misunderstanding. This practice results in the development of more *humility*. Even if you feel *confident* that you are perceiving accurately, with *humility* you will be more inclined to do the inner work of consciousness and less inclined to practice the power tactic of *blame*. The process of exploration can then be undertaken with the proper focus on claiming full responsibility.

Checking out perceptions also may mean asking about the validity of memories that pertain to your experience. Memories were stored at various times in your development, using the perceptions you made at the time of those events. Memories are second hand perceptions, making them highly questionable. The original perception was tinted, the storage capabilities in your memory system may have been unskilled, the original event may have been connected to other experiences, and your memory system may have had a different internal agenda occurring that led you to remember inaccurately.

Memories need updating often. As you gather greater information, and process it from a more mature level of development, your memories will change. There is no such thing as an absolutely true memory. *Humility* about your memories will increase as you *sincerely* seek your personal truth. Regardless of how *adamant* you feel about the accuracy of your memories, remember that your memories were constructed from your previous experiences, before you had the knowledge to check out your perceptions. So you probably constructed memories from faulty perceptions. As these memories become pertinent to your present experience, it is necessary to question their accuracy.

Checking out your memories may mean taking any number of possible courses of action. Memories can be reconsidered internally using new information you may have gained. Memories can be questioned by comparing them to the memories of others who shared the same events. You can search for additional information in any records of the events in question, like photographs, diaries, letters, newspaper articles, family stories and records, and so on. Sometimes you can stimulate recollection of memories, which may have been repressed or forgotten, by putting yourself in the environment of that previous memory and noticing your present experience.

In all cases, remember that the information you come up with may also be faulty. Memory is an unreliable record-keeping system, whether it is yours or someone else's. Take any new information with a measure of *skepticism*, just as you would your own memory. At the same time, *trust* in your truth. Even if all the pieces do not fit together perfectly, listen to what your truth is saying to you. Your relationship with your own personal truth is foremost. As in any relationship, *consideration* and *trust* are key elements to its growth.

**Exploration**

Having done everything possible to check out your perceptions, you can now begin to explore your emotions as the second step of the Pathway of Emotions. Be *patient*. Be *sensitive* to your experience. *Appreciate* all of the discoveries for their uniqueness, regardless of their level of *pleasantness*. Feel and get to know the feeling. Feel and explore. Feel and explore. Feel and explore. Make friends with every experience, intimate friends. Quell the screams of your *fearful* unconscious through your recommitment to your willingness. Look for ways to describe your experience, using great detail, using colorful and complete descriptions.

Some descriptions to begin looking for are: What does it feel like to have this experience? Is it more noticeable in one part of your awareness than in another? Can you feel the experience in specific parts of your body, such as your mouth, neck, throat, shoulders, hands, stomach, chest, anus, toes, feet? If you can locate specific body sites for an experience, then the next time you have this same body sensation you may also be feeling the same emotions.

What color does this experience remind you of? Is it light? Heavy? What is its texture? Does it bring up specific memories? Are there other associated emotions, like every time you feel *sadness* do you then also feel *scared*?

Of course, all of this exploration requires that you remain in the experience. You cannot turn emotional exploration into a cognitive exercise. If you do, then you are only exploring your thoughts. And you are gaining no more *familiarity* with your actual emotional experience.

At the same time, you need to process all of this emotional data through your great biocomputer, your brain. So the exercise is not completely non-cognitive. But to really explore and come to know any piece of emotional territory, you need to stay in the experience as completely as possible. This requires a re-affirmation of your first choice to be willing to feel. Heading for the *safety* of your cognitive abilities, and getting away from the emotion, is one technique of denial.

Feel the experience. Get to know it intimately. Name it. This requires having vocabulary that can adequately describe the emotion. Practice using new emotion words, so that you can expand your vocabulary to include more of your real experience. If someone was very unsophisticated about their emotions they might have only two words for them: *good* and *bad*. As sophistication is gained about their emotions, they might learn ten or twenty words that describe emotions. There are, literally, hundreds of words that describe emotional experiences.

When you were born, and before you began using denial for survival, you had the ability to feel all of the emotions in the spectrum. Now you can recover awareness of a large part of these emotions. It is your birthright, after all. So see how many of these emotions you can *relate* to. Use the list in **Appendix A** to measure your growth in your ability to feel all of your emotional experiences. See how it changes in a year or two, after you have practiced the Path of Emotion.

Think of the emotional skill of exploration as an adventurer would think of exploration. If you were dropped into the middle of a forest, you would need to first gather knowledge of your surroundings, before making any decisions in regard to your future behavior. If you were skilled in the ways of forests, you would probably decide to explore your surroundings in a systematic way.

You would get to know your immediate surroundings first, starting from where you were. You would build your knowledge from the center outwards, in concentric circles. You would register every landmark, and you would gain familiarity of the territory. In this way you would avoid the pitfalls and dangers of random choices. You would avoid the repetition of criss-crossing your efforts. You would come to know each tree, rock, hill, valley, quagmire and cliff.

Only after gaining comfort with your knowledge, would you be better able to make reasonable and informed choices about the destinations you may be seeking. Any choice you might try to make before you gain this familiarity from thorough exploration would be nothing more than a shot in the dark.

Exploration in an emotional sense is begun by asking yourself: "How do I feel?" It can be in reference to a specific event: "How did I feel when this happened?" Or it can be in reference to the present situation in your life: "How do I feel right now?"

Emotions rarely occur in pure, isolated form. Emotions almost always occur in combinations. Look for these combinations as you ask yourself how you feel. You may feel simultaneous emotions that seem contradictory, such as feeling *appreciative* and *angry* at the same time. Each experience in your life is a unique combination of emotions. These emotions combine to form a pattern, with a specific weave. An experience is adequately explored when you get a comprehensive picture of that experience. You identify the texture, the pattern, and the weave of the experience, like you would a tapestry. Register any landmarks you may find. Acquaint yourself with every shade and nuance. Note the quagmires and cliffs. Be an explorer of your experience.

When you are comfortable with this basic level of exploration of your experiences, there is still more exploration to learn. Ask yourself how you feel about each of the emotions you identified in the first level of exploration. "How do I feel about feeling *overlooked*?" "How do I feel about feeling *self-righteous*?" This then begins to clarify a second level of experience, which also forms into a tapestry with a unique weave, texture, and pattern.

This process of exploration can be repeated with as many as five or six levels of experience, maybe even more. That is to say, you may have this many different and distinct levels of emotional experience occurring simultaneously. When you are proficient at exploring your experience down through the various levels, you may come upon a discovery about yourself that is so enlightening that you are rendered nearly speechless and immobile. This epiphany is called an "Aha!" experience, because of the understanding it casts into many corners of your previous experiences.

You may also come across the same Aha! many different times, starting from seemingly different situations and experiences. When you begin to recognize familiar "Aha's!" at very profound levels of experience, then you have identified a "core experience."

Core experiences are those that are at the center of all your experiences. For example, on the surface, you might feel *unheard* and *angry* and *disappointed* and *discouraged*. As you track your experience to the second level you might feel *embarrassed, apologetic, self-centered*, and *mean*. At still another level you may begin to recognize a sense of *unworthiness, pretense, deceit*, and *dishonesty*. As you explore it to even another level, e.g. "How do I feel about feeling *unworthiness*", you may recall a nagging sense of "*not-good-enough, never-good-enough, you're-a-nobody*" kinds of messages that usually preceded your father going away from you. This is labeled "*abandonment*," and is a common core experience, present in some degree in nearly all humans. This, then, in this example, would be a core experience. Core experiences are always present, even if they are sometimes buried under several levels of more superficial experience.

You have core issues. All humans do. These are the issues that are constantly with you. They usually number no more than ten or twelve, but half that amount is more common. In any given experience, exploration is complete when you have explored your experience wide enough and deep enough to identify which of your core issues are coming into play at this time. Core issues often feel so *large* that they cannot be readily seen, as if they exceed your field of vision. Once identified, you will wonder how you could have missed them. Since they are always present, they show up in every situation in your life. Learning to see and know your core issues, is one of the rewards of doing your work consistently and depthfully. What used to be invisible to you becomes obvious, and extraordinarily useful in using that experience to choose your behavior consciously.

Exploration of this quality does not happen quickly. It often takes someone years of skill development to be able to explore his or her emotional experience to this degree of clarity. Further, it probably will require the assistance of a professional psychotherapist to train you to this depth. Everyone needs psychotherapy if they are to claim their full self-responsibility and grow into higher consciousness. Psychotherapy is the only place, to date, where you can learn the emotional skills necessary to do this quality of self-discovery and self-cultivation. Hopefully some day these skills will be commonplace, and preclude the need for professional, individual training. Until then, one-to-one training by someone who knows and practices the emotional skills that lead to higher consciousness is necessary. Psychotherapy, also called professional counseling, is where you learn them.

You cannot put your life on hold while you take the time necessary to fully explore every situation. Although this would ensure speedy growth in consciousness if you could, realistically, you may be able to only commit an hour a day to thorough exploration of an experience. In this case, devote the effort to those situations that seem most *distressing* to you. Feel all of the situations in your life; remember willingness must be constant. But if you must ration your time for exploration, then choose the experiences of highest potential. Usually they are the most *painful*.

The more situations in your life that you fully explore, the easier it gets to do this work efficiently. Someone very skilled in the emotional aspect will be able to do this exploration in minutes, or maybe even seconds. But when you first begin to learn this skill, it requires a commitment of time, as well as effort. It may take you hours, days, or perhaps weeks to adequately explore an experience of high *distress*. Practice pays dearly. The more exploration you do of your emotional experiences the more familiar of the territory you become.

Exploration is not the mere labeling of experience. Tagging an experience with a name is not the same as coming to know that experience. Going back to our adventurer in the forest, her being able to identify this thing as a tree, or even identify it as an aspen tree, is not the same as her knowing the size, colors, markings, uniqueness, leaf pattern, angles, branches, age, etc., etc., etc., of that tree. In order for her to be able to know this tree she must spend adequate time with it. Do not mistake labeling for exploration.

Similarly, do not get lost in your *judgment* of any specific emotion. It really doesn't matter whether you *approve* of it or not. You have the same work to do in either case. If you identify an emotion within your experience that causes you *concern*, and you don't *like* the idea of you feeling this emotion, then regard it as our adventurer might regard a brambles. It is present. Your not *liking* it won't change that. It is part of the landscape, and your job is not to waste time considering whether it is a reasonable or justifiable part. Your job is to know it. Explore it with the same willingness you choose when you are exploring a more *acceptable* tree.

Partners in a relationship can be especially helpful in this process of exploration. Your partner can help you to focus on the areas of greatest *discomfort*. Your partner can ask you the questions that prompt your exploration, and lead you to the next level of exploration. Your partner can sometimes see your blindspots and be able to offer you information that you otherwise might have difficulty finding. Obviously this is a two-way street, and you can do the same for your partner. In this way you assist each other in your personal growth. More on this avenue to growth will be included in Chapter 12.

> *"I looked for God and found myself.*
> *I looked for myself and found God. "*
> (Hazrat Inayat Khan, Sufi founder)

Another helpful tool for exploration is the use of a personal journal. A journal is a collection of your writings, usually kept chronologically. A journal differs from a diary in that a diary is a record of the events of your life, whereas a journal is a description of the emotional experiences in your life. Journal writing helps you to build a strong link between your emotional aspect and your mental aspect. Thus, it helps you to increase your awareness of your emotions.

A journal is some of the most important work you will ever do in your life. It should be regarded as such. It is helpful to buy a plain paper book with a hardbound cover, perhaps one that has a picture of something *pleasing* to you on the cover. You are going to put you within those pages. Do not skimp on the extra dollar, or so, it might cost to acquire a journal book that *pleases* you to look at, and to hold, and to spend time in. It is not a work of art, yet. But after you explore your experiences within its pages, it will be.

You can also journal on a word processor or personal computer if you prefer. However, the look of a computerized journal is impersonal and indistinguishable from any other document you have there. When you work on paper you are investing your own handwriting, your physical effort as well as your mental effort. You create something that is entirely unique in the world. You can even add drawings in a journal book, or insert pictures. And the order in which you write can never be edited in an attempt to clean up the composition. The journal stays the way you originally worked through your awareness of your emotions. It reflects your stream of consciousness. In a computer you may have the tendency to rearrange thoughts and feelings to suit your ego. Either will do. But the handwritten, hardbound journal will present a more useful picture to you of yourself.

Eventually, your first journal will be joined by a second, and a third, and so on. With each journal you will become more proficient in exploring your emotions, and using them effectively. Your journal, then, becomes a record of your growth into higher consciousness. Many people are concerned with their apparent lack of growth, or slow growth, only to be astounded at how far they have come so quickly when they can review the history of their growth in their journal.

Although a journal is a useful record of your growth, its primary function is that of a training device. A journal trains your mind to pay attention to your emotions. In accomplishing this, a journal helps you to create the discipline of overriding your automatic and unconscious denial. Your journal will also help you to create a sense of control over the effects of your emotions. If you cannot find anything else to do with certain emotions, you can always write about them; explore them. Use words that best describe your experience; usually the stronger the emotion, the more *passionate* the writing. *Passionate* writing, in and of itself, is a worthwhile contribution to the world. Writing in your journal is a powerful and healing exercise.

When you work in a journal, it is helpful to create a discipline that works for you. Find a time every day when you can spend unhurried time exploring your emotional experiences. You may find it helpful to write during the same time every day: first thing upon rising; a midday pause for reflection; or an evening meditation. Fifteen to thirty minutes per sitting should be enough, unless you have many unresolved experiences that require more thorough review.

You can begin each entry by asking yourself, "What have I been feeling during the past 24 hours?" You may need to recount the specific events of the past day in order to remember the emotions that were raised. When you first begin journal writing, your primary purpose is just to become aware of the emotions you may have been ignoring. When you consistently ask your mind to recount the emotions of the previous day, it starts to get the message that it needs to pay attention to your experiences as they occur, so they can be recalled later.

By becoming aware of your emotional experiences, you will begin the process of learning how to use them more effectively. When you can recount most of the emotional experiences of the previous day, then continue on by asking yourself about second-tier experiences, as described above. How do you feel about those more-superficial emotions? Then, how do you feel about these? And so on. A journal can become one of your most important tools of self-exploration, if you use it in the spirit of *sincerely* seeking your truth.

One of the paramount conditions to establish for journal work is that of absolute privacy. In order to be able to use your journal to explore your emotions, it is essential that you *trust* that no one will violate the sanctity of your privacy. You should communicate, with those with whom you share your living space, about the importance of privacy, mutual *respect* and *trust*. No one should ever look into your journal unless you ask him or her to view certain entries. To do so is to violate your deepest vulnerabilities. You will not give yourself the permission necessary to feel emotions that may be *uncomfortable* for you, or those that you *fear* would insult others around you, if you *fear* those individuals might discover you. Nor would you give yourself permission to try out different feelings, or thoughts, or possible behaviors, in route to a more conscious conclusion, if you *fear* someone might read them and assume they are your conclusions.

Similarly, you should never use your journal as a means of communication. To write something in your journal, and leave it laying around, *hoping* that someone specific will pick it up and read how you feel, is a *passive-aggressive* ploy that is sure to backfire. If you need to write to someone, instead of talking directly, then write a letter that is separate from your journal. Do not jeopardize the sanctity of your journal, and lose it as an effective tool for your own exploration.

▲

## Chapter 9
## Claiming Your Personal Truth

*A*s you explore your emotional experience thoroughly, the sources of your emotion begin to emerge. You become so *familiar* with the terrain of your experience that you begin to connect certain emotions with other specific emotions. The threads of commonality begin to appear. Underlying beliefs, values, perceptions and early life experience become more visible, a visibility that is only made possible with thorough exploration. If these underlying sources of emotion are not yet visible, then there has been insufficient exploration. The measure of how much exploration is necessary is defined by the emergence of the sources of emotion.

You do not need to move too quickly in attempting to find the sources of your emotion. Jumping ahead to the search for underlying sources is sometimes another ploy of the unconscious to avoid the actual experience, by getting into the more *comfortable* area of thinking about that experience. No truth is gained, despite the appearance of having done all the steps. The emotions first must be felt, and explored, and made *familiar*. You must know your experience before you try to gain truth from it.

Thus far, on the Path of Emotion, you have committed to your willingness to feel all that you feel. You paid attention to your emotional experience in this specific situation. You allowed yourself to feel it completely, and you explored these emotions. You explored the emotions through several levels of experience, and you begin to identify a sense of commonality with many other experiences.

Now ask yourself, "What beliefs are present in this experience?" "Are there values of mine that are involved here?" "Is this a matter of how I perceive my world?" Is this experience reflective of my early life experience?" Reflect on your inner voice. Stop analyzing. Allow your soft, intuitive voice to speak. You are not looking for solutions. You are creating resolution. The answers are created internally.

Self-questioning is a learned skill involved in reviewing your emotional source. Even if you are using someone else to assist you in your exploration, their questions and perceptions are merely stimulating your own self-questioning. The first of these questions, by necessity, is always, "Do I really want to know what is true for me, regardless of how this might change my current understanding of my world? Am I committed to knowing my truth?"

If the honest response to this is "No," then you have identified your primary issue. It is called avoidance. Avoidance differs from denial in that it allows you to be aware of your emotions, even though you then refuse to deal with them responsibly. Denial keeps you from this awareness in the first place.

In avoidance, you feel the experience, but then you choose to not use it to make internal changes. Avoidance reflects an investment in your current understanding of yourself and your world that is so high that you would rather live with *pain* and *disharmony*, than have to deal with truth.

Avoidance is an effort to maintain the status quo, a dedication to not "rocking the boat." To avoid your truth, you must, by definition, choose to ignore what you have already become aware of. It is the clearest cause of ignorance: to ignore information that is available. Avoidance is a dynamic used in an effort to not claim responsibility for your own emotions, to blame others.

Avoidance sentences you to a lifetime identity as a victim. In your *desire* for internal *peace* and *harmony,* you must try to change those around you to behave in certain ways, so as not to invite your feelings of *discomfort.* You make yourself a victim of their behavior. Avoidance is the classical Sisyphean struggle: an eternity of rolling the bolder up the hill, only to have it roll back down just before reaching the top.

You have the right to continuously create such a reality. But the question must be, "Why would you want to?" Avoidance is a decision to live with your *discomfort* and ineffectiveness, because you never get to the true source of your experience, where you can change it. Avoidance is an issue. It is not a skill, like denial. It does not serve your survival. It does not effectively create any useful reality. It is not effective in any constructive way. It only creates more and more of the *pain* and *suffering* you already experience. You have the right to do so, but why?

Enlightenment is the ultimate level of consciousness as a human BEing. To realize higher consciousness, you must learn the lessons that block your growth. To learn your lessons, you must embrace them. Embracing your lessons requires you to feel your experience. Personal growth is only possible when you feel your emotions and seek to learn the lessons involved in that experience. Your unconscious will constantly act to steer you away from your emotions, and into safer ground. People around you, who are also *afraid* to seek their lessons and do not want you to "rock their boat", will invite you to ignore your experience, ignore your truth, and live in an illusion of *safety.* You are the only one who makes the choice to listen to the calling of your birthright, a realization of enlightenment. Avoidance of your experience, and therefore avoidance of your truth, will keep you forever in the mundane struggles of lower consciousness.

The following story, from American Indian teachings, describes the challenges each of us must face in the process of knowing our personal truth and choosing to live consistently with it. It is the story of "Jumping Mouse", from the book, Seven Arrows by Hyemeyohsts Storm, to whom we wish to express our sincere gratitude for his counsel and his permission to use this traditional story. Thank you, Wolf!

■■■■■■■■■■■■■■■■■■■■■■■■■■■■■■■■■■■■■■■■■■■■■■■■■■■■■■

[Author's note] "Within Seven Arrows, and particularly within the old Stories, the words to which the Teller would have given inflections are capitalized. These words are symbolic Teachers, and it is very important that you approach them symbolically rather than literally. These capitalized words may sometimes seem inconsistent, but do not be confused by this. The Coyote is known among the People as a gentle trickster, and his Way is a part of Sun Dance Learning."[5]

## Jumping Mouse

Soon half a dozen children were clustered around the Story-Teller. He lit his Pipe and began:

Once there was a Mouse."

He was a Busy Mouse, Searching Everywhere, Touching his Whiskers to the Grass, and Looking. He was Busy as all Mice are, Busy with Mice things. But Once in a while he would Hear an odd sound. He would Lift his Head, Squinting hard to See, his Whiskers Wiggling in the Air, and he would Wonder. One Day he scurried up to a fellow Mouse and asked him, "Do you Hear a Roaring in your Ears, my Brother?"

"No, no," answered the Other Mouse, not Lifting his Busy Nose from the Ground. "I Hear Nothing. I am Busy now. Talk to me Later."

He asked Another Mouse the same Question and the Mouse

---

[5] Storm, Hyemeyohsts, Seven Arrows, Ballantine Books, ©1972

Looked at him Strangely. "Are you foolish in your Head? What sound?" he asked and Slipped into a Hole in a Fallen Cottonwood Tree.

The Little Mouse shrugged his Whiskers and Busied himself again, Determined to Forget the Whole Matter. But there was that Roaring again. It was faint, very faint, but it was there! One Day, he Decided to investigate the Sound just a little. Leaving the Other Busy Mice, he scurried a little Way away and Listened again. There it was! He was Listening hard when suddenly, Someone said Hello.

"Hello, little Brother," the Voice said, and Mouse almost Jumped right Out of his Skin. He Arched his Back and Tail and was about to Run.

"Hello," again said the Voice. "It is I, Brother Raccoon." And sure enough, It was! "What are you Doing Here all by yourself, little Brother?" asked the Raccoon. The Mouse blushed, and put his Nose almost to the Ground. "I Hear a Roaring in my Ears and I am Investigating it," he answered timidly.

"A Roaring in your Ears?" replied the Raccoon as he Sat Down with him. "What you Hear, little Brother, is the River."

"The River?" Mouse asked curiously. "What is a River?"

"Walk with me and I will Show you the River," Raccoon said.

Little Mouse was terribly Afraid, but he was Determined to Find Out Once and for All about the Roaring. "I can Return to my Work," he thought, "after this thing is Settled, and possibly this thing may Aid me in All my Busy Examining and Collecting. And my Brothers All said it was Nothing. I will Show them. I will Ask Raccoon to Return with me and I will have Proof."

"All right Raccoon, my Brother," said Mouse. "Lead on to the River. I will Walk with you."

Little Mouse Walked with Raccoon. His little Heart was Pounding in his Breast. The Raccoon was Taking him upon Strange Paths and Little Mouse Smelled the scent of many things that had Gone by this Way. Many times he became so Frightened he almost Turned Back. Finally, they Came to the River! It was Huge and Breathtaking, Deep and Clear in Places, and Murky in Others. Little Mouse was unable to See Across it because it was so Great. It Roared, Sang, Cried, and Thundered on its Course. Little Mouse Saw Great and Little Pieces of the World Carried Along on its Surface.

"It is Powerful!" little Mouse said, Fumbling for Words.

"It is a Great thing," answered the Raccoon, "but here, let me Introduce you to a Friend."

In a Smoother, Shallower Place was a Lily Pad, Bright and Green. Sitting upon it was a Frog, almost as Green as the Pad it sat on. The Frog's White Belly stood out Clearly.

"Hello, little Brother," said the Frog. "Welcome to the River."

"I must Leave you Now," cut in Raccoon, "but do not Fear, little Brother, for Frog will Care for you Now." And Raccoon Left, Looking along the River Bank for Food that he might Wash and Eat.

Little Mouse Approached the Water and Looked into it. he saw a Frightened Mouse Reflected there.

"Who are you?" Little Mouse asked the Reflection. "Are you not Afraid being that Far out into the Great River?"

"No," answered the Frog, "I am not Afraid. I have been Given the Gift from Birth to Live both Above and Within the River. When Winter Man Comes and Freezes this Medicine, I cannot be Seen. But all the while Thunderbird Flies, I am here. To visit me, One must Come when the World is Green. I, my Brother, am the Keeper of the Water."

"Amazing!" little Mouse said at last, again Fumbling for Words.

"Would you like to have some Medicine Power?" Frog asked.

"Medicine Power? Me?" asked little Mouse, "Yes, yes! If it is Possible."

"Then Crouch as Low as you Can, and then Jump as High as You are Able! You will have your Medicine!" Frog said.

Little Mouse did as he was Instructed. He Crouched as Low as he Could and Jumped. And when he did, his Eyes Saw the Sacred Mountains.

Little Mouse could hardly Believe his Eyes. But there They were! But then he Fell back to Earth, and he Landed in the River!

Little Mouse became Frightened and Scrambled back to the Bank. He was Wet and Frightened nearly to Death.

"You have Tricked me," little Mouse Screamed at the Frog!

"Wait," said the Frog. "You are not Harmed. Do not let your Fear and Anger Blind you. What did you See?"

"I," Mouse stammered, "I, I Saw the Sacred Mountains!"

"And you have a New Name!" Frog said. "It is Jumping Mouse."

"Thank you. Thank you," Jumping Mouse said, and Thanked him again. "I want to Return to my People and Tell them of this thing that has Happened to me."

"Go. Go then," Frog said. "Return to your People. It is Easy to Find them. Keep the Sound of the Medicine River to the Back of your

Head. Go Opposite to the Sound and you will Find your Brother Mice."

Jumping Mouse Returned to the World of the Mice. But he Found Disappointment. No One would Listen to him. And because he was Wet, and had no Way of explaining it because there had been no Rain, many of the other Mice were Afraid of him. They believed he had been Spat from the Mouth of Another Animal that had Tried to Eat him. And they all Knew that if he had not been Food for the One who Wanted him, then he must also be Poison for them.

Jumping Mouse Lived again among his People, but he could not Forget his Vision of the Sacred Mountains.

The Memory Burned in the Mind and Heart of Jumping Mouse, and One Day he Went to the Edge of the River Place.... Jumping Mouse went to the Edge of the Place of Mice and Looked out onto the Prairie. He Looked up for Eagles. The Sky was Full of many Spots, each One an Eagle. But he was Determined to Go to the Sacred Mountains. He Gathered All of his Courage and Ran just as Fast as he Could onto the Prairie. His little Heart Pounded with Excitement and Fear.

He Ran until he Came to a Stand of Sage. He was Resting and trying to Catch his Breath when he Saw an Old Mouse. The Patch of Sage Old Mouse Lived in was a Haven for Mice. Seeds were Plentiful and there was Nesting Material and many things to be Busy with.

"Hello," said Old Mouse. "Welcome."

Jumping Mouse was Amazed. Such a Place and such a Mouse. "You are Truly a great Mouse," Jumping Mouse said with all the Respect he could Find. "This is Truly a Wonderful Place. And the Eagles cannot See you here, either," Jumping Mouse said.

"Yes," said Old Mouse, "and One can See All the Beings of the Prairie here: the Buffalo, Antelope, Rabbit, and Coyote, One can See them All from here and Know their Names."

"That is Marvelous," Jumping Mouse said. "Can you also See the River and the Great Mountains?"

"Yes and No," Old Mouse Said with Conviction. "I know there is the Great River. But I am Afraid that the Great Mountains are only a Myth. Forget your Passion to See Them and Stay here with me. There is Everything you Want here, and it is a Good Place to Be."

"How can he Say such a thing?" Thought Jumping Mouse. "The Medicine of the Sacred Mountains is Nothing One can Forget."

"Thank you very much for the Meal you have Shared with me, Old Mouse, and for sharing your Great Home," Jumping Mouse said. "But I must Seek the Mountains."

"You are a Foolish Mouse to Leave here. There is Danger on the Prairie! Just Look up there!" Old Mouse said, with even more Conviction. "See all those Spots! They are Eagles, and they will Catch you!"

It was hard for Jumping Mouse to Leave, but he Gathered his Determination and Ran hard Again. The Ground was Rough. But he Arched his Tail and Ran with All his Might. He could Feel the Shadows of the Spots upon his Back as he Ran. All those Spots! Finally he Ran into a Stand of Chokecherries. Jumping Mouse could hardly Believe his Eyes. It was Cool there and very Spacious. There was Water, Cherries and Seeds to Eat, Grasses to Gather for Nests, Holes to be Explored and many, many Other Busy Things to do. And there were a great many things to Gather.

He was Investigating his New Domain when he Heard very Heavy Breathing. He Quickly Investigated the Sound and Discovered its Source. It was a Great Mound of Hair with Black Horns. It was a Great Buffalo. Jumping Mouse could hardly Believe the Greatness of the Being he saw Lying there before him. He was so large that Jumping Mouse could have Crawled into One of his Great Horns. "Such a Magnificent BEing," Thought Jumping Mouse, and he Crept Closer.

"Hello, my Brother," said the Buffalo. "Thank you for Visiting me."

"Hello, Great Being," said Jumping Mouse. "Why are you Lying here?"

"I am Sick and I am Dying," the Buffalo said, "And my Medicine has Told me that only the Eye of a Mouse can Heal me. But little Brother, there is no such Thing as a Mouse."

Jumping Mouse was Shocked. "One of my Eyes!" he Thought, "One of my Tiny Eyes." He Scurried back into the Stand of Chokecherries. But the Breathing came Harder and Slower.

"He will Die," Thought Jumping Mouse, "If I do not Give him my Eye. He is too Great a Being to Let Die."

He Went Back to where the Buffalo Lay and Spoke. "I am a Mouse," he said with a Shaky Voice. "And you, my Brother, are a Great Being. I cannot Let you Die. I have Two Eyes, so you may have One of them."

The minute he had Said it, Jumping Mouse's Eye Flew Out of his Head and the Buffalo was Made Whole. The Buffalo Jumped to his Feet, Shaking Jumping Mouse's Whole World.

"Thank you, my little Brother," said the Buffalo. "I know of your Quest for the Sacred Mountains and of your Visit to the River. You have Given me Life so that I may Give-Away to the People. I will be your Brother Forever. Run under my Belly and I will Take you right to the Foot of the Sacred Mountains, and you need not Fear the Spots. The Eagles cannot See you while you Run under Me. All they will See will be the Back of a Buffalo. I am of the Prairie and I will Fall on you if I Try to Go up the Mountains."

Little Mouse Ran under the Buffalo, Secure and Hidden from the Spots, but with only One Eye it was Frightening. The Buffalo's Great Hooves Shook the Whole World each time he took a Step. Finally they Came to a Place and the Buffalo Stopped.

"This is Where I must Leave you, little Brother," said the Buffalo.

"Thank you very much," said Jumping Mouse. "But you Know, it was very Frightening Running under you with only One Eye. I was Constantly in Fear of your Great Earth-Shaking Hooves."

"Your Fear was for Nothing," said Buffalo. "For my Way of Walking is the Sun Dance Way, and I Always Know where my Hooves will Fall. I now must Return to the Prairie, my Brother. You can Always Find me there."

Jumping Mouse Immediately Began to Investigate his New Surroundings. There were even more things here than in the Other Places, Busier things, and an Abundance of Seeds and Other things Mice Like. In his Investigation of these things, Suddenly he Ran upon a Gray Wolf who was Sitting there doing absolutely Nothing.

"Hello, Brother Wolf," Jumping Mouse said.

The Wolf's Ears Came Alert and his Eyes Shone. "Wolf! Wolf! Yes, that is what I am, I am a Wolf!" But then his mind Dimmed again and it was not long before he Sat Quietly again, completely without Memory as to who he was. Each time Jumping Mouse Reminded him who he was, he became Excited with the News, but soon would Forget again.

"Such a Great Being," thought Jumping Mouse, "but he has no Memory."

Jumping Mouse Went to the Center of the New Place and was Quiet. He listened for a very long time to the Beating of his Heart. Then Suddenly he Made up his Mind. He Scurried back to where the Wolf Sat and he Spoke.

"Brother Wolf," Jumping Mouse said ....

"Wolf! Wolf," said the Wolf ....

"Please, Brother Wolf," said Jumping Mouse, "Please Listen to me. I Know what will Heal you. It is One of my Eyes. And I Want to Give it to you. You are a Greater BEing than I. I am only a Mouse. Please Take it."

When Jumping Mouse Stopped Speaking his Eye Flew out of his Head and the Wolf was made Whole.

Tears Fell down the Cheeks of the Wolf, but his little Brother could not See them, for Now he was Blind.

"You are a Great Brother," said the Wolf, "for Now I have my Memory. But Now you are Blind. I am the Guide into the Sacred Mountains. I will Take you there. There is a Great Medicine Lake there. The most Beautiful Lake in the World. All the World is Reflected there. The People, the Lodges of the People, and All the Beings of the Prairies and the Skies."

"Please Take me there," Jumping Mouse said.

The Wolf Guided him through the Pines to the Medicine Lake. Jumping Mouse Drank the Water from the Lake. The Wolf Described the Beauty to him.

"I must Leave you here," said Wolf, "for I must Return so that I may Guide Others, but I will Remain with you as long as you Like."

"Thank you, my Brother," said Jumping Mouse. "But although I am Frightened to be Alone, I Know you must Go so that you may Show Others the Way to this Place." Jumping Mouse Sat there Trembling in Fear. It was no use Running, for he was Blind, but he Knew an Eagle would Find him Here. He Felt a Shadow on his Back and Heard the Sound that Eagles Make. He Braced himself for the Shock. And the Eagle Hit! Jumping Mouse went to Sleep.

Then he Woke Up. The surprise of being Alive was Great, but Now he could See! Everything was Blurry, but the Colors were Beautiful.

"I can See! I can See!" said Jumping Mouse over again and again.

A Blurry Shape Came toward Jumping Mouse. Jumping Mouse Squinted hard but the Shape Remained a Blur.

"Hello, Brother," a Voice said. "Do you Want some Medicine?"

"Some Medicine for me?" asked Jumping Mouse. "Yes! Yes!"

"Then Crouch down as Low as you Can," the Voice said, "and Jump as High as you Can."

Jumping Mouse did as he was Instructed. He Crouched as Low as he Could and Jumped! The Wind Caught him and Carried him Higher.

"Do not be Afraid," the Voice called to him. "Hang on to the

Wind and Trust!"
          Jumping Mouse did. He Closed his Eyes and Hung on to the
Wind and it Carried him Higher and Higher. Jumping Mouse Opened his
Eyes and they were Clear, and the Higher he Went the Clearer they
Became. Jumping Mouse Saw his Old Friend upon a Lily Pad on the
Beautiful Medicine Lake. It was the Frog.
          "You have a New Name," called the Frog. "You are Eagle!"

          [In American Indian spirituality, the eagle is the highest form of
BEing, enlightenment.]

■■■■■■■■■■■■■■■■■■■■■■■■■■■■■■■■■■■■■■■■■■■■■■■■■■■■■

## Claiming Personal Truth

          If the honest response to "Do I really want to know my truth?" is
"I do," then first comes the elusive work of knowing your personal truth.
Since each emotion is an unconscious expression, it is through exploring
your emotions that your beliefs, your values, your perceptions, and your
early life experience become visible to your consciousness. Each
experience results from its own combination of sources. Most of your
sources are hidden in your unconscious. Using the iceberg model, perhaps
as much as 89% of your emotional sources are unconscious. It is through
your current experience, each and every moment, that you have access to
a piece of your unconscious that was not previously available to you.
          By following the path of your emotion, you are traveling into
your previously undiscovered or unclaimed part of you. You will see
pieces that have not been previously visible. You can know yourself to
greater depth. You can even make changes to how you experience the
world.
          Claiming your personal truth, which is the inherent opportunity
in any given experience, first necessitates uncovering which of your
beliefs, values, perceptions and early life experiences have contributed to
these emotions. From the awareness of your core issues identified by
thoroughly exploring your experience, you can now inquire of yourself
which emotional sources might be relevant in this experience.
          A partner, who is perceptive and supportive and willing to
engage at this level, is especially helpful in this process. Your partner can
see the obvious, when you might not. They can see your blindspots that
are very difficult for you to see, no matter how quickly you turn to try to

see them. They can ask the simple questions that you might tend to overlook. A partner in truth is one of the remarkable blessings of a conscious relationship.

But even if you do not have this blessing of an intimate partner, you can proceed with this step in claiming your personal truth. After checking out your perceptions and exploring your emotions, ask yourself the questions of discovery, noted above. From your quiet, inner voice, you will probably have an intuitive response to follow. If not, you will have to go through a process of elimination by asking yourself investigative questions about possible sources related to the experience at hand.

"Does this have to do with a belief about .....?" "Could this be related to a belief about ....?" "What are my values regarding ....?" "Am I missing or disregarding a value of mine concerning ...?" Always pause long enough to listen for the intuitive responses. Perhaps you hear voices inside of you that are repeating specific and familiar messages, such as, "Don't ....," "You shouldn't ....," "You ought to ....," "Mom says ....," etc. Some values are so common, or so ingrained, that they are easily overlooked, such as, "Respect your elders."

This process usually cannot be learned from a book, including this one. A professional counselor acts like a life-partner by asking you pertinent questions, making observations, offering perceptions, and guiding you to your own discovery. The essence of psychotherapy is to assist you in discovering, reviewing, updating and claiming your personal truth. The skills involved in claiming your truth, while they can be described here, can not adequately be taught and learned within the covers of a book.

If you have trouble grasping these skills in reading these pages do not *despair*. Most people will probably need the guidance of a good therapist to learn how to rummage around in their beliefs, values, perceptions and early life experience. Psychotherapy is the only place where these skills are taught, if they are not adequately modeled by healthy parents and caretakers. It is for this reason that we emphatically say that psychotherapy is something that everyone needs, not just the emotionally *distressed*. You serve yourself well, your partners, your children, and the world in general, by seeking out a good therapist who can teach you these skills. Psychotherapy truly is for everyone.

Listen to your inner voice during this process of examining your emotional sources. It will give you hints as to the nature of your truth that is emerging now. After the belief, value, perception, or early life

experience is identified, you still must claim what is currently true for
you. Just because you have a belief does not make it a true belief for you.
Just because you have a value does not mean you have it in its proper
priority order. A perception may be falsely coloring an experience. Or a
memory of your early life may have been created through someone else's
agenda, and lack factual basis.

"Claiming your truth," means continuously working on
accepting full responsibility for your beliefs, values, perceptions and
early life experience; all of them, including those that you are conscious
of and those that are still in the unconscious. There are a few steps that
help you to do this.

You must become aware of your beliefs, values, perceptions and
early life experience that underlie every emotional experience. Test them
for their current truthfulness. Make any changes that may be necessary.
Only then can you fully claim that emotional source as yours. This
becomes part of your personal truth, a truth that you can stand up for;
emotional experiences from which you accept fully.

> *"You shall know the truth,*
> *and the truth shall set you free. "*
> (Jesus of Nazareth, reported by John)

After you have identified the beliefs, values, perception or early
life experience that created the emotional experience you are exploring,
you can test it for its truthfulness. To do so, you use *The Ring of Truth*, as
presented in Chapter 4, to feel if it is true for you. If it rings true when
you state the belief aloud and listen to your body's response, then you
have only to claim to it. You claim a truth by declaring it to the inner
universe of you.

"This is my belief. No one besides me is responsible for my
belief. It is true for me. I can no longer deny, avoid, or ignore it. I
understand that I will be creating certain emotional experiences because I
hold this belief. So be it. This is me, as I understand me to be at this point
in my self-awareness. I take full responsibility for this belief and all of its
implications in my life, foreseen and unforeseen. This is part of my

personal truth. I own it."
    Claiming truth is not merely an oath. The act of owning the truth is more than just repeating words. It is not a casual act. It is not an act where you get it done and put it behind you. Owning a truth is a process that continues forever, or until it is no longer true. It is the complete *acceptance* of this part of who you are. It is a heartfelt embrace of your essence, your soul, your BEing. Just as though you were looking in a mirror and recognizing your reflection, you own a truth because it is the reality of who you are. In owning a truth, you confirm what is; not because you necessarily want it to be this way, or because you think you will gain from it, but simply because it is The Way It Is; it is The Way. Truth is truth; anything less is untrue, false.
    If an identified belief (or value, perception, early life experience) does not ring true, then you must determine if any part of it is true. Would it ring true if you alter the statement somewhat, or does it ring completely false? If it is partially true, then change the statement of the belief so that it more brings you closer to the ring of full truth. Re-test it using the same skill. Continue making adjustments to the statement until you have a "rings true" experience. Then claim it, fully owning your belief, knowing that it will create certain emotional experiences for you.
    If *The Ring of Truth* results in the experience of "*that doesn't ring true at all*," then the next step in claiming your truth would be to formulate and verbalize the new belief regarding these core issues that does ring true. Identifying the new belief however, will not automatically make the old belief disappear. It will make it easier for you to deal with the next experience in which this old belief creates an *uncomfortable* emotion.
    When you explore a subsequent experience created by the old belief, you will be able to more quickly identify the core issues, remember the old belief and re-validate your new belief, thus changing the emotional experience rather quickly. The more you create the new emotional experience, the more a pattern will develop. The experience created by the old false belief will gradually be replaced by the experience of the true belief.
    It is in this way that you create new ways of experiencing the world. As you update and change your personal truth you will experience a different emotional pattern. Remember that you cannot correctly call the sources of your emotion your "Personal Truth" until you have explored and claimed all of your experience that is available to your consciousness, past and present. It is not your truth until you claim it,

taking full responsibility for it. Before then, before it is your personal truth, it is merely the source of your emotion, conscious and unconscious. Remember, too, taking responsibility for yourself is the core lesson of the emotional aspect of your BEing.

The work of uncovering beliefs, values, perceptions and early life experience inevitably involves confronting some emotional sources that have sacred status assigned to them. Some sources have a belief attached to them that protects them from questioning. For example, it may seem *disrespectful* to question certain messages from your parents. If you believe "honoring your parents" means you cannot question their teachings, then doing so can feel quite *threatening*, or even *sinful*.

However, if you are ever to fully claim your responsibility, then you must choose the willingness to feel these experiences. If such a double-guarded experience occurs, then explore how you feel about the "guard" belief, and test it, using the ring of truth. "I believe that it is *disrespectful* to my parent (or to my religion, or to my profession, etc.), to question their teaching." (Pause and listen.) Modify, update and claim the belief that rings true for you.

You can not hope to claim your personal truth if you declare certain parts of your life as "off limits." Those beliefs, values, perceptions and early life experiences that you hold as sacred and therefore untouchable, are some of the most important to challenge. Perhaps you do this with your religious or moral teachings, or with certain relationships, or with political beliefs. You cannot have "sacred cows," those parts of your life that you have declared untouchable, and live in truth.

All of the sources underlying your emotional experiences must pass the test of the Ring of Truth. If they do not, or they have never been tested, then they are creating internal *disharmony* and external contradiction. You cannot excuse any of your beliefs from this test and still expect to claim full self-responsibility. You would limit your growth in consciousness at the very level where you became aware of your untouchable source.

Occasionally, when testing a belief for truthfulness, you do not get any clear response from your body. It may be that the belief you are testing is actually a collection of beliefs, some of which contradict others. Try to separate out the various beliefs and test them individually. State each belief in a single simple sentence that your body can resonate to. If you use paragraphs to describe your belief, you will probably inadvertently include more than one belief. And your body won't know which one to tune in to.

Although this discussion primarily has been referring to claiming your beliefs, the same skill is used to claim your values, perceptions and early life experiences, which are no less important than beliefs, and also cause specific emotional experiences. The only difference in the application of *The Ring of Truth* to values is to compare one value to another in terms of priority. "My value of completing every task that I undertake is more important than my value of showing my *love* for my son by attending his performance." In this way, you listen to your organic response to the statement you are testing. If it does not ring true, then try it again, reversing the priority. Testing all your values for their relative priority, and thus their current truth, allows you to establish a clear list of your values according to their priority.

Perceptions are similarly tested for their validity and their effect in your life. In addition to checking-out perceptions with the other person, you will have the ability to use your ring of truth as a final filter for determining the validity of a perception. Even if a thousand people tell you that you are misperceiving a situation, the only measure that counts is your internal ring of truth. Of course, it might behoove you to consider the opinions of those around you, but it is your truth that requires claiming responsibility for. If you try to accept that you must be wrong because your consultants have told you so, then you will not be able to accept the responsibility necessary for choosing truthful behavior.

If your perception remains at odds with the reports of those whom you consulted, continue to checkout the differences between your perception and their report. How can two people, both of whom are intelligent and sincere and honest and committed to their personal truth, see a situation so differently? With enough mutual exploration, and with full commitment to truth, perceptions can usually find mutual agreement. But again, in the final tally, you can only claim responsibility for your perceptions. Even if totally inaccurate, they are still your perceptions, and you are going to have to live with the emotions and the consequences of your behavior that are driven by your perception.

Early life experiences are usually based in memories, faulty devices for storing your experience. Like perceptions, you can only claim responsibility for how you know your experience. Early life experiences may not even be clear memories. They may, instead, be a feeling or a deduction of how things must have been, based on how you react now to certain situations. All early life experiences must also pass the ring of truth if you are to claim responsibility for them. To test these experiences, or memories of experiences, or feelings, or deductions, you must first attempt to gather as much information as possible.

Gathering information about your early life experience requires adopting the attitude of an investigator. You ask questions of those who might have knowledge of your experience; all the time remembering that the information you receive will always be skewed by that person's issues.

Since you are not attempting to find fault or place blame on others for your present experience, there will be no cause for *guardedness* or *defensiveness*. Unfortunately, however, more times than not, family and friends will view family investigation as a *threat* to their reality. Proceed with sensitivity to their reactions, but proceed anyway. You are endeavoring to make conscious that which is mostly unconscious so that you can claim responsibility for your personal truth. Resistance, ruffled feathers, and strained relationships pale in importance. You are not responsible for their emotions, which are created by their internal sources. If you determine that Uncle Bob was a lecherous alcoholic, who threatened the sanctity of your body or your *safety*, even if everyone else invites you to believe he was just a "good-time Joe", it is your experience that you must claim in your personal truth. It is your truth that you are responsible for, not anyone else's.

Knowing and claiming your personal truth does not automatically clear up your life. But it does give you a solid basis for the emotions you create and the behavioral decisions you make. Following this clarity, you will still be confronted with the choice of whether or not to behave according to what is true for you. And the choice to behave truthfully often is not an easy one. Frequently, those around you don't *like* your choice of behavior. They might *reject* you; perhaps even *persecute* you. Only you can decide where living according to your truth falls in your list of values. What is true for you concerning your personal truth?

When your behavior is not consistent with your personal truth, you create internal *disharmony*, and sentence yourself to the experiences of lower levels of consciousness.

▲

# Chapter 10
# Truthful Behavior

o choose behavior that is in full accordance with your personal truth in every situation, in every moment, is the essence of full self-responsibility and therefore, full consciousness. It is your behavior that impacts the universe. Any behavior that is less than fully responsible, that is less than fully conscious, is a risky investment. For every behavior has consequences.

The behavior you choose, whether through consciousness or unconsciousness, is like tossing a pebble into a pond. Every behavior, as every pebble, sends out ripples. The ripples from the pebble are usually more visible than the ripples from behaviors. But visible or not, there are ripples. With the pebble we may be able to predict what some of the consequences from the ripples will be. They may wash ashore here and there. They may rearrange the shore somewhat. They may be just one more in a never-ending series of washings that occur on a rock. There will probably be consequences from some ripples that you cannot predict. But there is no such thing as a pebble without ripples.

Likewise, there is no such thing as a behavior without consequences. There will be consequences from every behavior. In claiming full responsibility for yourself, you must be prepared to claim full responsibility for all of the consequences of your behavior. You have the choice whether you will make conscious choices, and therefore create consequences for which you can claim responsibility, or you will make unconscious choices, which also create consequences for which you are responsible, but probably have difficulty claiming. You are equally responsible for the consequences in either choice.

Just like the ripples from the pebble however, it is not likely that you will be able to predict all of the consequences of your behavior. This can be a *frightening* proposition for many people, "What? I am responsible for all of the consequences of my behavior? Even if I didn't mean for that to happen? Even if I didn't know that would happen?"

This *fear* of creating unforeseen or unintended consequences can lead to *immobilization* in some people. You might be so *afraid* of taking responsibility for the consequences of your behavior that you are *reluctant* to act at all. But choosing to not act, whether through consciousness or unconsciousness, is a choice none-the-less, a choice in behavior that has consequences for which you are responsible.

It is an illusion that you can play it *safe,* and not make any consequences in the world, by not acting. If the prospect of having to claim full responsibility for the consequences of your behavior is *overwhelming* or *immobilizing*, remind yourself that you are always behaving, and therefore always creating consequences. The only difference is whether you will choose to create consequences that occur from conscious behavior, or you create consequences that occur from unconscious behavior.

An unconscious choice is called a reaction. When you react to your world you immediately make an unconscious, pre-programmed choice about your behavior. This behavior creates consequences. If you react again to the new consequences, you have again behaved unconsciously. By continuing to react, create consequences, and react again, you create a pattern of consequences. People talk about having "bad luck" or "can't get ahead" or "there aren't any good men left in the world" or "this job sucks." Sometimes people refer to the pattern as "destiny," "fated by the stars," or "things just happened." This pattern of consequences usually feels like something outside of you is controlling your world.

The fact is you have created your world, and you have been creating it all along. This is done through a pattern of unconscious reactions. You certainly haven't controlled your destiny through awareness, but control it you did. Through this cycle of unconscious reactions, you create the same *unpleasant* experiences repeatedly.

> *"Knowing others is intelligence;*
> *knowing yourself is true wisdom. "*
> (Lao Tzu)

A reaction looks like this in the Sequence of BEing:
**100% Self-Responsibility**

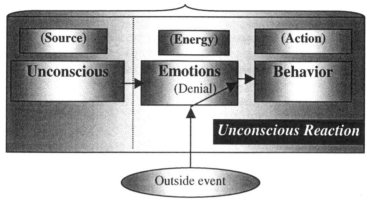

**Sequence of BEing (9)**

Not knowing about the sources of your emotion, and not knowing about the limits of your responsibility, you went into a continuous pattern of feeling-and-doing, feeling-and-doing, feeling-and-doing. By unconsciously reacting to the events and situations in your life, you have created the pattern that exists now. Regardless of how well you used your other three aspects, mental (thinking), physical (activity), or spiritual (praying), if you did not realize and claim your personal truth before you chose behavior, it was still an unconscious reaction. Since personal truth can only be accessed through your emotion, denial of your emotion kept you forever cycling in that pattern of unconscious reaction.

As a method of selecting behavior, unconscious reaction has severe limitations. Through reacting you can only create consequences in patterns that repeat themselves. This usually becomes visible after you have been through several relationships that all begin to look alike; or several past jobs all look the same as the present one; or you see yourself parenting your children the same way your parents treated you, and you swore you'd be different; or a multitude of other similar patterns you create through unconscious reactions.

When you react, unconsciously, to outside events in your world, you tend to create feelings of *isolation, inadequacy, separation, anger, blame, discontent, "quiet desperation",* and *internal disharmony.* When you do not behave, consciously, according to your personal truth, you create *disharmony.*

Choosing your behavior in a way that allows you to freely create your future is the goal of seeking consciousness. Instead of repeating the same emotionally *distressing* patterns, you have the ability to create your world according to your truth. This is accomplished by inserting a Loop of Consciousness into your Sequence of BEing. This loop began with your choice to be willing to feel and to deal, and continued with exploration of all of your emotions, their various levels, and your core experiences. Then you were able to identify, update and claim your personal truth.

These are the first three steps in the Path of Emotion: Willingness, Exploration, and Claiming Personal Truth. The final step in this path is Choosing Truthful Behavior. All four steps are required to complete a conscious experience.

If you complete only the first step, then you will probably become emotionally *raw.* That is, you will experience emotional *overload.* It was this condition that originally led you to shut down your emotions back when you were a child who felt the full spectrum of emotion, but you didn't find acceptance for all you felt nor training in how to deal with what you felt. Willingness, without the following three steps is *exhausting,* and eventually deadly.

If you only choose to be willing to feel, and you explore your feelings, the first two steps, you will create an infinite loop of processing your life's experiences. This, too, is usually *exhausting* and leads you to change your environment in *hoping* to change the loop of your processing. You might seek a new location, a new partner, a new job, or anything that looks like it will give you *relief* from the infinite processing.

If you practice only willingness, and exploration, and claiming your personal truth you will begin to experience the "prize." It is here that you begin to know, to understand, to see, to be aware, to "*grok*" (a term invented by Robert Heinlein in his book, Stranger In A Strange Land, to connote full and complete integration of something into your BEing). If you complete the first three steps in the Path of Emotion you will achieve a higher level of awareness. But awareness is only a booby prize. It feels like you have won something, but the *thrill* soon wears off when you realize nothing has changed. Awareness is not consciousness. It is only a step along the way. Awareness does not become consciousness until it is put into action. It is only through conscious behavior, behavior that is consistent with your personal truth, that you can begin to claim consciousness.

When you choose your behavior consciously, based in your personal truth, you are responding to the outside events in your world, instead of reacting. Responding means having the capability of making a choice based in your truth, for which you can claim responsibility for the consequences.

In each experience, you cannot consciously choose your behavior until you have claimed your personal truth. You cannot claim your personal truth until you have thoroughly explored your emotions. You cannot explore your emotions unless you consciously choose to be willing to feel and to deal. Each step in the Path of Emotions is dependent upon the step before. None of the steps can be minimized or skipped. No one step is more important than the others. They all must be completed, and they must be completed in order: Willingness, Exploration, Claiming Personal Truth, and Truthful Behavior.

By inserting this Loop of Consciousness into your Sequence of BEing you will create a different emotional experience, one that reflects your new level of self-responsibility. By using this loop of consciousness, you will make the energy of your emotions available to you. It is yours. You created the energy. You claimed the responsibility. You no longer blame, nor credit, anyone else for your experience.

A conscious response looks like this in the Sequence of BEing:

**100% Self-Responsibility**

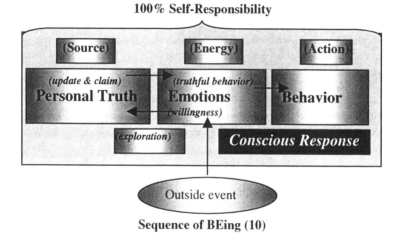

**Sequence of BEing (10)**

With the emotional energy you create you are able to choose how you want to behave in the world to effectively deal with your emotion. The process of making this choice consciously is the skill that completes the Path of Emotion and turns awareness into consciousness.

**Truthful Behavior**

Conscious responses involve the skill of deliberately choosing your behavior so that it puts your personal truth into action. This deliberation is slow and sometimes tedious when you first begin to practice the skill. But as you become proficient at going through the process, you will be able to choose your behavior consciously in a fraction of a second.

Ken Keyes, Jr., in his book, <u>Handbook To Higher Consciousness</u>, describes affirmations that are relevant to specific skills in the pursuit of higher consciousness. He calls these "The Twelve Pathways to Unconditional Love and Happiness." The Ninth of these is especially helpful as you learn and begin to use the skill of Conscious Choice Making. It says:

> *"I act freely when I am tuned-in, centered, and loving,*
> *but if possible I avoid acting when I am emotionally upset*
> *and depriving myself of the wisdom that flows*
> *from love and expanded consciousness."*
>
> (Ken Keyes, Jr.)

As you learn to follow the Path of Emotion, and create your world through self-responsibility for personal truth and truthful behavior, remember to choose to not act, as much as possible, before you have allowed yourself to work each step of the Path. Conscious Choice Making takes time to complete. Allow yourself the time necessary to practice this skill at every opportunity, every experience.

> *"Can you remain unmoving*
> *until the right action arises by itself?"*
>
> (Lao Tzu)

After you have claimed your personal truth, choosing truthful behavior involves using the skill of Conscious Choice Making. Begin by feeling what your intuition tells you about your behavior. In every situation you will be inclined to behave in a certain way. It is in this exercise that you begin to develop a relationship of *trust* between your rational self, which has been diligently seeking your personal truth, and your intuition. Your intuition is part of you, and it can be an extremely helpful part if you learn how to listen to it and use it in making conscious choices.

If you do not have a sense of direction about your behavior, an intuitive inclination to behave a certain way, then it is very likely that you have not completed the work of exploration and claiming your personal truth. When you know your truth, behavior has a large measure of self-evidence. "Doing the right thing" has been a common phrase for this self-evidence, although this usually has an authoritative "should" connected to it rather than being based in personal truth.

You cannot do the skill of conscious choice making merely as an intellectual exercise (except perhaps to discover that you really are making choices, conscious and unconscious, in every moment of your life). You cannot make conscious choices, by definition, unless you have claimed your personal truth up to that moment. And you cannot claim your personal truth unless you have thoroughly explored your emotions and the core issues you are dealing with in that moment. And you cannot adequately explore your emotions unless you are fully willing to feel them all and to deal with them all. Step one, then step two, then three, then and only then can you engage in making conscious choices. By the time you complete the first three steps in the Path of Emotion your intuition will probably be screaming certain behavioral choices to you.

Hear what your intuition says about the "right" or "necessary" course of behavior in regard to this situation and experience. Your internal voice will tell you that you need to behave in a certain way, a behavior that rings true. "I need to go talk with Bob about my experiences from the incident at yesterday's meeting." "I should quit this job and go do what I've always wanted to do." "Jessi needs to know how I feel about her behavior. I'd better tell her." "I want to move to Michigan." "I can no longer participate in that mission. It's time for me to choose a different way." "That just doesn't feel right." "I'd really like to get to know him better." And so on...

Taking your lead from your intuition, or from its self-evidence, compose a statement describing the behavior. For example, "I will leave this job." It helps, when practicing this skill, to write this statement down. Circle the statement about this behavior. Surround the circled statement with other circles, one for each of the negative or *unpleasant* consequences that are possible as a result of actually doing this behavior. Write these *unpleasant* consequences within each circle.

Neatness and exact organization do not matter. What does matter is that you paint a picture of the choice you face. Here is a picture of what the exercise of Conscious Choice-Making will look like as you practice it on paper:

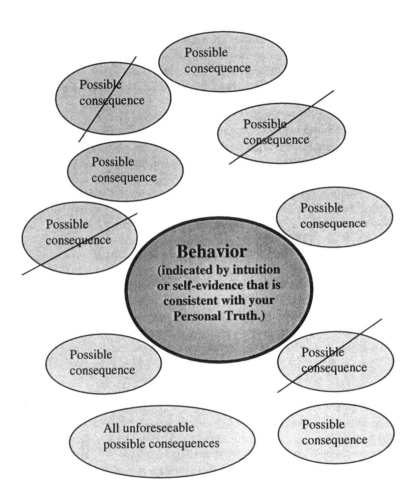

(Reminder: Include only the possible *__unpleasant__* consequences.)
**Conscious Choice-Making**

Taking each consequence, one-at-a-time, in no specific order, ask yourself the question, "If this consequence to my behavior should occur, am I willing to deal with it?" If your honest answer is, "Yes, I am willing to deal with this consequence, should it occur," then you can cross it off your picture. Those consequences that you are willing to deal with present no difficulty to your claiming responsibility for that choice of behavior. Remember that to "deal" with something means to begin the Path of Emotions all over again: Willingness to feel, Exploration, etc.

Notice that the question is not, "What consequences do you want to have happen," nor is it, "What is the probability of any particular consequence." Even if there is only one chance in a billion of a specific consequence actually occurring, as long as there is any chance of it occurring, you must be prepared to accept responsibility for this consequence and deal with it. The questions of "What you want?" or "What is the probability?" are not useful in you choosing behavior that is in accordance with your truth.

For example, every year skiers die on the ski slopes of Colorado. Given the number of skiers and the number of days they ski, the percentage of skier deaths is very small. Further, if you always ski under control you can minimize the possibility of such a tragedy even more. But deaths do occur, sometimes even to experienced skiers. To ignore this possibility as a consequence to the choice to ski is to not fully claim responsibility for your behavior. "What do you want to do," and "What is the probability of a certain consequence," are not useful questions at this step in your conscious process. Similar examples can be made of your choice to drive an automobile, or to fly in an airplane. Remember that the only relevant question you need to ask yourself is, "Am I willing to deal with this possible consequence, should it occur?"

Truthful behavior has nothing to do with a measurement of the "pros" vs. the "cons", nor of a measurement of probability. There may be only one reason to do something, and a thousand reasons not to do it, and still it may be truthful behavior. The only question of relevance is, "Am I willing to deal with this consequence, should it occur?"

If your honest answer to this question about any consequence is "No, I am not willing to deal with this possible consequence of my behavior." then this indicates to you what you need to deal with before you could choose this behavior in consciousness. You would begin the Path of Emotion in regard to this new situation: Willingness to feel and deal, Exploration of all of your Emotions, Claiming Your Personal Truth, and Choosing Truthful Behavior.

Discovering a possible consequence that you are not willing to deal with does not mean the end of your original issue. It merely means that you have another issue to deal with before you can complete the first one. So you begin the work on the second, keeping the first one on hold only as long as necessary to do the second. The exploration of the second issue may be as simple as gathering information or becoming educated as to how to deal with the consequence that presented a barrier. For example, a potential parent may balk at making the decision to bring a child into the world when they consider the possible consequence that child may be born with a physical impairment. Information about resources and education about caring for the child may alleviate the parent's *fears* of the unknown. When the parent is willing to deal with that possible consequence, should it occur, then the parent can return to the original issue of bringing a child into the world.

When you first begin this process of cleaning up and claiming your life, you may find yourself interrupted several times before completing the Path about the first issue. One issue often leads to another, and another, and so on. This is why psychotherapy is so helpful, especially in the beginning stages. It helps you to "houseclean" all those unresolved issues you have been carrying around for many years.

If there is a conflict between the behaviors suggested to you by your intuition, which you feel, and by those suggested by your mind, which you think, then you have a second issue on which to work the Path. How do you feel about this apparent conflict between your intuition and your mind? Willingness. Exploration. Claim Personal Truth. Truthful Behavior. Work to resolve this apparent conflict between the various parts of you. The more you can learn to trust your intuition, then the more it can serve you in those occasions when you do not have the time necessary to fully explore, claim, and choose conscious behavior.

To make the exercise complete there is one more consideration to conscious choice making. After having imagined all of the possible consequences to a specific course of behavior, you must always add one more. Include with the picture of possible consequences the additional category of "all those possible consequences that I can not foresee." It is often these unforeseeable consequences that test your commitment to claiming full responsibility for your behavior.

"Unforeseeable consequences" is an acknowledgment to yourself that, being human, you are not omniscient. In most situations you cannot predict all of the consequences that may result from your behavior. Just like the ripples in the pond, you will not know where all of your behavior will impact all of the areas of your world. Since your vision is limited in this manner you must prepare yourself for dealing with consequences of your behavior that are unpredictable or unforeseeable.

You can do this by considering "unforeseeable consequences" as another possible consequence of your behavior in the exercise of Conscious Choice-Making. Ask yourself, "Am I willing to feel and to deal with the possibility that unforeseeable consequences may result from my behavior?" If you can accept responsibility for this consequence of your behavior, then it does not present an issue that prevents you from choosing this behavior. If you are not willing to feel and deal with possible consequences that are unforeseeable, then you cannot responsibly choose this behavior in truth.

By using the skill of Conscious Choice Making you can literally put one foot in front of the other in choosing your behavior as you travel through your world. If you can claim full responsibility for your behavior, each and every moment, then you begin to create a world that is in alignment with your personal truth.

■■■■■■■■■■■■■■■■■■■■■■■■■■■■■■■■■■■■■■■■■■■■■■■■■■■■■

### Unforeseen Consequences

One child was seven, the other was three, on that spring morning when the mother was trying to get to the office on time to greet her clients. She had several stops to make along the way, and the schedule was carefully planned: daycare, elementary school, office. On the way out of the house and to the car, the seven year old spotted two fuzzy caterpillars moving across the driveway and stopped to watch.

This activity was not budgeted into the schedule. The mother's reaction would have been to take the child by the arm, rush him into the car, grumble at him about the *stresses* of juggling a career with parenthood and expound the need for his cooperation for her to be on time, and *wonder* aloud her *regrets* for attempting to do both. All of her *disharmony* would have seemingly arisen from the child's behavior of pausing to satisfy a *curiosity* about his world.

That's what would have happened had not the mother paused, paused for consciousness. Instead of creating a *hurtful* explosion, she tuned into having used the skill of Conscious Choice Making to make her decision about bringing a child into the world eight years earlier. The exercise looked like this, showing that each possible consequence was felt, explored and claimed:

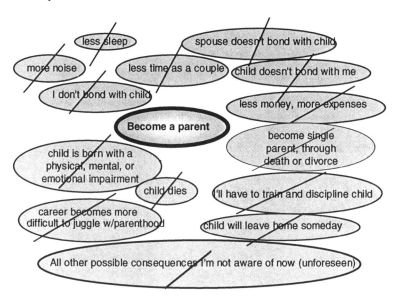

**Conscious Choice to Become A Parent**

The mother realized, with a chuckle, that this was one of those possible consequences that was not foreseen. She had no way of knowing eight years earlier that she would be standing beside a child viewing a caterpillar on the way to being late to the office. She tuned into the fact that her being in this situation was a result of her having made a choice to be a parent. Her *distress* was not the child's fault. He was being a normal child who was *interested* in his world. She made the choice to be a parent, with all of its possible consequences. She made a choice, and here was one of the consequences of her choice.

As she acknowledged this responsibility, she relieved her *distress* and *disharmony*, and opened up more creative modes of BEing. She no longer felt *like a victim*. She felt like a *choice-maker* who had made a conscious choice, a choice she would make again, and now was realizing some of that responsibility. She quickly ran inside the house, got a mason jar and poked holes in the lid. She hurried back out, plucked some grass with one hand and the caterpillar with the other, and passed it to her child as he got into the car, suggesting he now had something to take for show-and-tell at school.

■■■■■■■■■■■■■■■■■■■■■■■■■■■■■■■■■■■■■■■■■■■■■■■■■■■

     If all of the consequences of a specific behavior are *acceptable*, according to your truth, then whatever occurs from your behavior will be in alignment. Consequences are not measured according to your *desires*, or according to the law of averages or probability. The only meaningful measurement of consequences of your behavior is whether you are willing to claim responsibility for them. And this is done according to your personal truth, using the skill of Conscious Choice-Making, as a last step to using the Path of Emotion. A Sequence of BEing that reflects the additional step of consequences © is below.

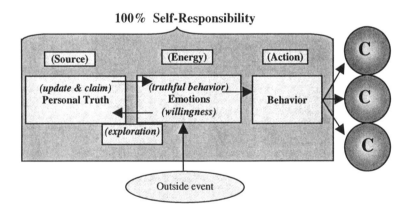

**100% Self-Responsibility**

**Sequence of BEing (11)**

     A final clarification is called for here, concerning responsibility for the consequences of your behavior. Common language refers to the need to "take responsibility for the consequences of your actions." It is a lesson that is taught to children by all good parents. It is at the heart of criminal rehabilitation. It is a message that encourages one to pause and reflect about consequences before acting. It is not a bad or wrong message. It is merely an elementary message in the claiming of self-responsibility.

What is proposed here is a fine-tuning of the concept of self-responsibility. If you choose behavior that is consistent with your personal truth, then you have already claimed full self-responsibility for your behavior. The question of responsibility needs to be answered before there are consequences. The issue of responsibility for the consequence to a particular behavior only has relevance in a remedial sort of way. It is trying to become aware after the fact, when the awareness was needed before the behavior was made. The old message about responsibility reflects the awareness that comes after you have already done some sort of unconscious behavior. In the pursuit of higher consciousness, this reflection must occur prior to expending energy.

You are absolutely responsible for your behavior, your emotions, and your personal truth. Responsibility for the consequences of your behavior is moot, and has no real answer. You are completely responsible for your behavior. No doubt about it, you have complete control over how you behave, and thus must accept complete responsibility for it. In choosing behavior that is consistent with your personal truth, using Conscious Choice-Making, you claim responsibility for your choice by confirming your willingness to deal with any possible consequences of your behavior, including any that might be unforeseeable. But once you behave, once you commit an act, the actual consequences that occur may not be entirely of your doing.

This is a fine point of responsibility, and it is not intended to be a tool for those who are *reluctant* to claim responsibility. To be clear, you must claim full responsibility for your behavior, which includes being willing to deal with any possible consequence, in order to make conscious choices about your behavior. Like the ripples on the pond, however, there may be energies or currents running from some other source that conflict with, alter, impede, enhance, or in some other way change, the energy that you put forth into the world through your behavior.

The energy that you put forth, in the form of your behavior (behavior includes thoughts, acts, postures, expressions, and anything that uses energy from you), is not the only source of energy in your world. The behaviors of others are also putting forth energies. The pebbles they toss also make ripples. Sometimes your behavior will seem like it is the only source of energy to a given situation. More often it will be only one of many sources. In most situations you will not know whether you are the only source, or just one of many. Claim full responsibility for your behavior. Responsibility for the consequences, then, is superfluous.

The consequences of a behavior can be likened to your shadow. Is it necessary or helpful to consider if you are responsible for your shadow if you have already claimed full responsibility for your body, which existed before the shadow? The question is moot, since you have already accepted responsibility for the object that is reflected as a shadow. Further, since the shadow could not exist unless there were some other form of energy, such as the sun or a bright light, whatever measure taken for responsibility for the shadow would have to include that energy source. And perhaps the humidity or particulate matter in the air affects the quality of the shadow. And perhaps several different sources of light are casting many different shadows, blurring the lines between each one. Isn't the pursuit of the question of who or what is responsible for the shadow a koan, a question with no answer?

Full self-responsibility is 100% self-responsibility for all of your behavior, all of your emotions, and all of your personal truth. It is the central lesson on the emotional aspect of your BEing. Get this lesson, and your level of consciousness will not be limited by your development on the emotional aspect. You will be creating your world in accordance with your personal truth.

▲

# Part III:  Lessons for Growth

# Chapter 11
# Personal Truth and Levels of Consciousness

*O*nce again, in each experience you cannot consciously choose your behavior until you have claimed your personal truth. You cannot claim your personal truth until you have thoroughly explored your emotions. You cannot explore your emotions unless you consciously choose to be willing to feel all that you feel.

BEing more truthful is the lesson available to you with every emotional experience. When you do not behave consistent with your personal truth, you create *disharmony*. The level of *disharmony* you create depends upon how many times you have previously been faced with the opportunity to discover and commit to your truth, but have made other choices.

If you exercise denial of your emotions, or employ avoidance of them, then you miss the opportunities presented to you in each experience for the unfolding of your personal truth. While the immediate result of this may be a feeling of *relief* for having been spared the inconvenience of "having to deal with something," the long-term effect is the accumulation of unlearned lessons.

This has at various times been referred to as "unfinished business," "emotional baggage," "psychoneuroses," "unresolved issues," "stress," or "repression." It can be recognized internally as any number of prevailing emotions, such as *depression* or *anxiety*, that constitute what is referred to as your mood. Unlearned lessons always show themselves in the more highly charged situations in your life.

Your lessons present themselves in all of the situations and events of your life. The first time a lesson is presented to you it usually comes as a slight tap on the door of your consciousness. If you accept it and deal with it, using the Path of Emotion, then it is a lesson learned. If you do not listen to the tap then you are creating the necessity for a second delivery.

The second time a lesson is presented to you it comes as a gentle pat. Again, your acceptance and dealing with it are what determine whether it is a lesson learned or unlearned. Unlearned lessons continue to repeat themselves, with increasing severity. The third presentation may be a knock, the fourth a pound, and so on. With repeated refusals to accept and deal with a lesson, through denial or avoidance, you will inevitably create the need for great drama in the presentation of your lessons. This is nothing more than the proverbial "large stick over the donkey's head" in order to get your attention.

Here is an example of a common pattern of denial or avoidance leading to increasingly dramatic presentations of a lesson.

■■■■■■■■■■■■■■■■■■■■■■■■■■■■■■■■■■■■■■■■■■■■■■■■■■■■■■

## In Denial

A 42 year-old woman discounts her own needs in lieu of her partner's. She knows this about herself when she pauses long enough to reflect on her life. But she makes the choice to ignore (avoidance) this nagging assessment (the slight tap). She has always believed it was right for her to sacrifice herself for her partner. She tells herself that her behavior is good, even though she continues to have that nagging self-assessment. She justifies it by telling herself, "Oh, he will start to pay attention to me soon."

Her friends tell her she is neglecting herself (the gentle pat), but feeling *noble*, she ignores the message. Her partner is becoming more demanding and demeaning. He wants the house cleaner, the food more appetizing, and the laundry sharper. Perhaps he even derides her for not bringing home more money. Her mother suggests to her one day that they should get counseling for their marriage problems (the knock), but she discounts her mother's suggestion by comparing the cost of counseling to their already *stressful* financial condition. "That's the last thing I need to do, to spend more money on myself."

During one of their arguments, her partner pushes her down (the pound). She knows things are not good for them, but she continues to ignore her internal message that she is not attending to her own needs. She rationalizes his outburst, "Oh, he didn't mean to hurt me, and I know he is sorry for it."

■■■■■■■■■■■■■■■■■■■■■■■■■■■■■■■■■■■■■■■■■■■■■■■■■■■■■■

You can see how this woman has had a slight tap, a gentle pat, a knock, and a pound on the door of her consciousness. It is not hard to imagine how the next presentation of her lesson might be a "large stick over her head." Each presentation was merely an opportunity for her to put her attention on her experience so that she might update and claim her truth and make conscious, and therefore self-responsible, choices.

Some people even fail to take notice of the presence of a lesson when they get hit with the "big stick." These people require that their messages come to them in even more dramatic fashion: getting "hit by a truck," "hit by a train," "having the bomb dropped on them," "hitting the bottom of the barrel," "WWIII," are some of the idioms used to express these more dramatic presentations.

Such is the essence of life crises. When you repeatedly refuse to deal with your lessons as they are presented to you, then you create the need for great disruption and *disharmony* to get your attention. Alcoholism, drug abuse, multiple failed relationships, identity crises, suicidal thoughts and actions, violent relationships: these are some, but not all, of the types of crises that are creations of unlearned lessons. Embrace and deal with the lesson, and the need for dramatic presentation is no longer necessary.

Or course, some people like to have drama in their lives. They like to "keep the pot stirred," to mix things up frequently. They justify this *desire* as adding spice to life. So their relationships are frequently in flux: up and down, hot and cold, calm and frenzied. They keep all areas of their lives in turmoil. The one thing they *fear* most is *boredom*, for this is equivalent to death to these people. Turmoil is proof positive of being alive. For this person, the need for drama is the lesson being presented. Even in these people's lives the intensity of the drama will increase until the lesson is learned.

It is the successful learning of your emotional lessons that creates growth on your emotional aspect, and thus allows your level of consciousness to rise. As presented in Chapter 3, **The Pyramid Model of Consciousness**, your level of consciousness is determined by the aspect of least development. Since the emotional aspect has not been a focus of training in most people's lives (as compared to the physical, mental, and spiritual aspects), this is the aspect that limits growth in consciousness for most people. Let's look at the various levels of consciousness, and the world you live in at each level, to see why you might want to pursue higher consciousness.

The concept of levels of consciousness has been part of Eastern philosophies for thousands of years. There, they are commonly known as chakras. While this has previously implied a level of spiritual awakening, it is now necessary to broaden and separate the aspects into four in order to put into everyday life the evolution to enlightenment, and allow the general population, East and West, to rise to a new level of consciousness.

The great spiritual teachers from the East, primarily India, who came to the West during the twentieth century, introduced the concept to the United States and the rest of the western world. Swami Muktananda, Mahareshi Mahesh Yogi, Paramahansa Yogananda, Swami Vishnu-devananda, Swami Satchidananda, Yogi Amrit Desai, Swami Rama, B.K.S. Iyengar, Swami Vivekenanda, Krishnamurti, Shivabalayogi, Sri Chinmoy, Yogi Bhajan, Osho Rajneesh, Baba Hari Dass, Baba Ram Dass (an American who studied in India), Meher Baba, Swami Prabhupada, Pir Vilayat, and others all brought with them this wisdom and shared it with their followers in the West.[6]

At the same time there was a resurgence of spiritual seekers in the West who gleaned teachings from a variety of sources. What was previously a predominantly Christian society, with minority followings of Judaism, Santeria, and American Indian Spirituality, quickly diversified into a multi-religious culture which included Buddhism, Islam, Hinduism, Taoism, many smaller religions, and a large minority of non-defined spiritual seekers which later became grouped together under the umbrella title of New Age.

Ken Keyes, Jr. was the one who most clearly defined the concept of levels of consciousness in a way that could be understood by Westerners. The first twelve chapters of his 1971 book, Handbook to Higher Consciousness, are necessary reading for anyone who wants to probe further into this teaching. His translation of the specific levels of consciousness is incomparable for clarity and usefulness.

The following chart describes the terms used by various teachings to name the levels of consciousness. It also serves as a reminder that every level of consciousness is experienced on all four aspects of BEing.[7]

---

[6] (Note: The authors do not intend to be comprehensive in their presentation of all disciplines, merely illustrative. If you, as a reader, happen to be more sophisticated in your understanding of these teachings, please forgive any gross oversights.)

[7] Keyes, Ken Jr., Handbook To Higher Consciousness, Living Love Press, ©1972.

## Levels of Consciousness

| Level | Name (Raja-Yoga[8]) |
|---|---|
| 7 | Crown Chakra (Sahasrara) |
| 6 | Pineal Chakra ("3rd Eye") (Ajna) |
| 5 | Throat Chakra (Visuddha) |
| 4 | Heart Chakra (Anahata) |
| 3 | Solar Plexus (Manipura) |
| 2 | Navel Chakra (Svadhisthana) |
| 1 | Root Chakra (Muladhara) |

| Level | Name (Yogi Philosophy[9]) |
|---|---|
| 7 | Spirit |
| 6 | Spiritual-Mind |
| 5 | Intellect |
| 4 | Instinctive-Mind |
| 3 | Prana, or Vital Force |
| 2 | Astral Body |
| 1 | Physical Body |

| Level | Name (Ken Keyes, Jr.[10]) |
|---|---|
| 7 | Cosmic Consciousness Center |
| 6 | Conscious Awareness Center |
| 5 | Cornucopia Center |
| 4 | Love Center |
| 3 | Power Center |
| 2 | Sensation Center |
| 1 | Security Center |

| Level | Name (BTES) |
|---|---|
| 7 | Enlightenment |
| 6 | Union |
| 5 | Unity |
| 4 | Intimacy |
| 3 | Power |
| 2 | Sensation |
| 1 | Security |

---

[8] Raja Yoga,

[9] Yogi Ramacharaka, Fourteen Lessons in Yogi Philosophy and Oriental Occultism, The Yogi Publication Society, Chicago 10, IL, 1904.

[10] Keyes, Ken Jr., ibid.

## Lessons at Each Level of Consciousness

| Level | Aspect | | | |
|---|---|---|---|---|
| 7 | (Enlightenment = no separation of aspects) | | | |
| | **Physical** | **Mental** | **Emotional** | **Spiritual** [11] |
| *Central* *Lesson:* *Chi* | | *Discipline* | *Self-responsibility* | *Faith* |
| 6 | Energy Fields | Blending | Merge | Universalize |
| 5 | Flexibility | Wisdom, Tolerance | Compassion | Paradox Integration |
| 4 | Fitness, Health | Cooperation | Intimacy | Responsibility |
| 3 | Strength, Endurance | Achievement | Interpersonal Safety | Perspective |
| 2 | Pleasure, Desires | Striving | Sobriety, Moderation | Literal Interpretation |
| 1 | Base Needs | Single Goal | Survival, Security | Concrete Thinking |

11. Fowler, James W., Stages of Faith; The Psychology of Human Development and the Quest for Meaning, HarperCollins, ©1981.

## Common Emotional Experiences at Each Level of Consciousness

| Level | Emotional Experience |
|---|---|
| 7 | *kinship with all life, complete knowledge of all things, certainty of immortality, certainty of having always been and of being destined to always BE, absence of all fear, acquisition of certainty, trust, and confidence, love of all without distinction[12],* **BEing** |
| 6 | *attuned to the more subtle energies, complete connection to all life, a piece of the whole,* **unified** |
| 5 | *Full, complete, appreciation, purposeful, generous, valuable, understanding, love of life, humble, insightful, grateful,* **connected** |
| 4 | *cooperation, partnership, appreciation, respect, love, hope, beauty, satisfied, healthy, trust,* **intimacy** |
| 3 | *anger, competition, me vs. them, right vs. wrong, defensiveness, pride, good guys vs. bad guys, dominance vs. failure, rebelliousness, hate on-guard, suspicious, conditional pleasure, victimization,* **control,** |
| 2 | *lust,* **cravings,** *addictions, pursuit of higher highs, desire for more, lost, lack of purpose, anxiety, fleeting satisfaction* |
| 1 | *dependency, emotional poverty, generalized fear, compliance, degradation, desperation, survival orientation,* **unsafe,** *worry, depression, hopeless, constant fear for security* |

---

[12] Raja Yoga

In looking at the emotional experiences that predominate each level of consciousness it is not hard to see why Levels 1, 2 and 3 are referred to as the Lower Levels of Consciousness, while Levels 4, 5, 6 and 7 are called the Higher Levels of Consciousness. The lessons that are being presented at the Lower Levels are all consuming. The emotional experiences are mostly *uncomfortable* and *distressing*. And the purpose of your life there is defined in the narrowest of terms.

The Lower Levels of Consciousness often are experienced collectively, rather than any one of them singularly. The security, sensation and power experiences often overlap, and therefore can present a *confusing* picture of which level of consciousness you are living. But there is no mistaking that you are living in these Lower Levels of Consciousness. The *disharmony* in your life is evident in nearly all areas of your life. The lessons of these three levels need to be addressed simultaneously, which may explain why so many people seem to get stuck there.

In actuality, all people have lessons at all seven levels of consciousness simultaneously. But you cannot address the lessons at higher levels until you have mastered the lessons of lower levels. Which level of consciousness you live in is not a matter of immediate decision on your part. While the experiences of the higher levels are generally *preferred*, you cannot arbitrarily choose those lessons over the lower levels. Consciousness is a building process. You cannot build the upper floors without first constructing the foundation and the lower floors.

> *"How do I know this is true?*
> *I look inside myself and see."*
> (Lao Tzu)

The lesson at every level of consciousness is to claim your personal truth and live according to it. As you do so, with 100% self-responsibility, you begin to develop mastery of the lessons at each level. Mastery does not mean that the issues of that level go away. The issues of each level of consciousness remain even after you have developed beyond that level. Mastery of those lessons merely means that you no longer create *disharmony* in your life when you encounter them, because you have immediate access to your truth and you are committed to living it. Remember, you create *disharmony* in your life when you do not behave according to your personal truth. When you are living truthfully, you do not create *disharmony*, even when you re-encounter an issue from a lower level of consciousness.

Denial and avoidance of your emotions keep you stuck in the lower levels of consciousness, creating the same lessons, over and over again, with increasing severity. How you do this is best illustrated in reference to a specific set of lessons in your life, such as in relationships. The next chapter addresses relationships. The mechanism by which you set up your lessons is explained there.

Following the path of your emotions, which begins with willingness to feel them, is how you can learn the lessons that are presented to you, and thus claim more and more of your personal truth and create a more conscious world through your behavior. While you may not be able to identify the level of consciousness where you live now, you can see where you have been in retrospect. Indeed, it serves no purpose other than ego satisfaction to spend much time attempting to identify your level of consciousness.

What is of utmost importance is that you remain focused on the lessons that are being presented to you right now, right where you are, always. Claim your personal truth and behave in a way that is consistent with your personal truth. BE There! Your level of consciousness will rise in turn. All attempts to be at a level of consciousness, other than where you truly are, are nothing more than self-delusion.

That said, it is sometimes *hopeful* to know that your current *suffering*, *confusion*, and *disharmony* are only temporary experiences necessary for you to receive and embrace your lessons. And that once the lessons of any level of consciousness are learned, then there will be a gradual shift in your experience toward the emotions that commonly predominate the next level of consciousness.

The following descriptions of the levels of consciousness offered by Ken Keyes, Jr. serve as a roadmap. In them you can find where you have been, and maybe where you are now. But it still remains that the only way you can chart your future is by being fully present with your immediate experience, using the Path of Emotion to feel, explore, claim, and choose. Anything else is more denial and/or avoidance, and will assure you of more severe presentations of your lessons.

## The Seven Centers of Consciousness[13]

**1. The Security Center.**
This Center makes you preoccupied with food, shelter, or whatever you equate with your personal security. This programming forces your consciousness to be dominated by your continuous battle to get "enough" from the world in order to feel secure.

**2. The Sensation Center.**
This Center is concerned with finding happiness in life by providing yourself with more and better pleasurable sensations and activities. For many people, sex is the most appealing of all sensations. Other addictive sensations may include the sound of music, the taste of food, etc.

**3. The Power Center.**
When your consciousness is focused on this Center, you are concerned with dominating people and situations and increasing your prestige, wealth, and pride --- in addition to thousands of more subtle forms of hierarchy, manipulation, and control.

**4. The Love Center.**
At this Center you are transcending subject-object relationships and are learning to see the world with the feelings and harmonies of flowing acceptance. You see yourself in everyone --- and everyone in yourself. You feel compassion for the suffering of those caught in the dramas of security, sensation, and power. You are beginning to love and accept everyone unconditionally --- even yourself.

**5. The Cornucopia Center.**
When your consciousness is illuminated by this Center, you experience the friendliness of the world you are creating. You begin to realize that you've always lived in a perfect world. To the degree that you still have addictions, the perfection lies in giving you the experience you need to get free of your emotion-backed demands. As you reprogram your addictions, the perfection will be experienced as a continuous enjoyment of the here and now in your life. As you become more loving and accepting, the world becomes a "horn of plenty" that gives you more than you need to be happy.

**6. The Conscious-Awareness Center.**
It is liberating to have a Center from which your Conscious-awareness watches your body and mind perform on the lower five centers. This is a meta-center from which you non-judgmentally witness the drama of your body and mind. From this Center of Centers, you learn to impartially observe your social roles and life games from a place that is free from fear and vulnerability.

**7. The Cosmic Consciousness Center.**
When you live fully in the Sixth Center of Consciousness, you are ready to transcend self-awareness and become pure awareness. At this ultimate level, you are one with everything --- you are love, peace, energy, beauty, wisdom, clarity, effectiveness, and oneness.

---

[13] Keyes, ibid.

Even if you cannot identify at which level of consciousness you currently live, there are some signs that indicate your current state of health on each aspect. These signs are not absolute predictors of your health. But taken as a complete picture they can give you some indication of how well you are succeeding with your efforts to claim yourself fully in all areas.

For example, most people have some understanding of their physical health. You generally know when you have an illness or a disease. Beyond the absence of disease, signs such as heart rate, blood pressure, and height-weight ratio are common ways to begin assessing your health. Blood chemistry, hair analysis, a food diary, body fluid and tissue checks are more sophisticated methods of assessing your physical health. These are all available through the services of your physician. All of the various disciplines of physical practitioners, whether they are a Medical Doctor (MD), Naturopathic Doctor (ND), Doctor of Chiropractic (DC), Doctor of Osteopathy (DO), Doctor of Acupuncture (Dipl. Ac.), Doctor of Homeopathy (DH), Doctor of Traditional Chinese Medicine (DTCM), or an assistant to any of these, are well schooled in making these types of assessments. Any problems in any of these signs can be addressed by the healer of your choice, the category of which extends far beyond the types of medical professionals listed here.

However, a full assessment of signs of physical health is not always necessary. A self-assessment can be made by regularly reviewing the basics of physical health. Are you sleeping well? Do you eat only healthy foods? Do you limit the amount and types of poisons you ingest, including alcohol, caffeine, medications, recreational drugs, nicotine, sugar, and exposure to sun or pollutants? Do you exercise your body adequately? Do you listen to your body and the messages it continually sends you? These simple assessments of physical signs will help you claim responsibility for your chi, for its nurturance and development.

A similar assessment can be made on your emotional aspect. One such assessment tool was created, again, by Ken Keyes, Jr. Written as affirmations of your intent to claim the consciousness that is rightfully yours, The Twelve Pathways[14] are a way to check with yourself to see how well you are dealing with your emotional experiences. Keyes suggests memorizing them and keeping them in your awareness to help you deal with every situation.

Some simpler tools for making a self-assessment about your

---

[14] Keyes, ibid.

emotional health are to honestly evaluate your abilities in certain areas. The first question to ask of yourself is, "Are you claiming full responsibility for yourself?" Since this is the key to emotional growth, and it is the central lesson of the emotional aspect through all levels of consciousness, then it is obvious that you will need to reflect on your ability to claim 100% self-responsibility. This includes all of your behavior, all of your emotions, and all of your personal truth.

Corollaries to this question are:

* Are you blaming anyone else for how you feel? (e.g. "He made me angry!")
* Do you credit anyone for how you feel? (e.g. "You make me feel wonderful!")
* Do you hold anyone beside yourself responsible for any of your behavior? (e.g. "I wouldn't have done it except they left me no choice!" or "They taught me to be this way.")
* Do you try to excuse yourself from the consequences of any of your behavior? (e.g. "I didn't mean for that to happen!")
* Are you blaming your parents for any of your beliefs or values? (e.g. "That's how I was trained to be!")
* Do you believe you cannot change who you are? (e.g. "That's just who I am, and I can't change it!")

Another measure of your emotional health can be taken by asking, "Can I identify and describe my core issues?" After all, it is these that determine your lessons, and therefore what experiences you are going to set up in your life. In a very practical sense these determine your identity. If you know your issues and can identify them whenever one of them appears, then you have an instantaneous understanding of "what's really going on here."

If you have ever gone to an event where they give you a stick-on nametag to wear so that others may know instantly who you are, then you can begin to see the helpfulness that knowing your own issues can provide. If you could list your issues and wear them as an identifying tag, then everyone with whom you came in contact would instantly know how to be helpful for you. And if everyone around you were equally disclosing of his or her issues, then you would instantly know how to relate to them in the most helpful manner. Of course, you would have to be willing to deal with your power and vulnerability issues.

Another ability to question of yourself is, "Can you find humor in your own issues when you catch yourself encountering them as a lesson?" Can you *appreciate* the perfection of the set-up, and catch the divine humor in the experience? Can you *love* yourself now, even as you are growing and learning? Can you make light of your own heaviness? The more you can smile at your own issues, the more you are finding the *humility* necessary for higher growth. As one person said, "This is schoolhouse Earth, learn your lessons. But don't forget that Earth is also the party planet. Make it *fun!*"

Children seem to know this instinctively when they come into this world. Their sense of *pleasure* and *joy* is often evident, even in those who are stricken with terrible tragedies. They can be quite helpful to you in creating *fun*, if you take the time to tune in to what they already know. They know how to look at events with *wonder* and *awe*. They aren't completely *afraid* of their emotions. They deny their emotions only when they need to do so in an effort to survive in their environment. They know how to receive what comes, without having *expectations* of how it should be packaged. They have a *thirst* for experience, and they embrace the very idea of change and newness that must accompany every experience.

This, then is one of the measures in your self-assessment of your emotional health. Can you *enjoy* and participate in the energy of children? Can you *appreciate* the wisdom that they brought with them into the world? Can you learn about Godly things from them, as well as teach them earthly things?

> "*Lest you become like a child,*
> *you will never enter the kingdom of heaven.*"
> (Jesus of Nazareth, reported by Matthew)

Another assessment tool is to ponder the changes you witness in yourself as you claim more of your responsibility. Can you see your old dynamics? Can you see how far you have come? Can you recognize your *clarity* with your issues now, compared to the *confusion* you felt when you were previously *lost* in your issues?

Last, and most important, are you able to be present in every situation by being fully aware of what you feel, claiming your personal truth, and make conscious decisions about your behavior? By following the Path of Emotion with every experience, every situation, you will learn your lessons, claim self-responsibility, and allow yourself to rise naturally in consciousness. As you increase your emotional skills, the emotional aspect of your BEing will no longer be the limiting factor to your growth in consciousness. As you master the emotional aspect then your lessons will appear on one of the other three aspects of BEing, necessitating a focus on those skills and central lessons, along with continuing emotional growth, to allow consciousness growth.

Next we will look at one of the most universal emotionally *troublesome* situations in the lives of adults, and how to begin your exploration of it. The experiences from early life are often difficult to integrate in a useful way, so many people try to ignore them (i.e. avoidance), or they make them into something they were not in order to feel *okay* about them (i.e. denial). In an effort to "get on with adulthood" they carry this unintegrated experience into their romantic relationships, and create something *disappointing* or even *regrettable*. Then in following their programming, they pass on to their children many of the same *troublesome* experiences. Childhood experiences, romantic relationships, and parenting: Let's look at the middle one of these three phases of development, and how you can claim full responsibility for yourself and create consciously what you truly want in a relationship.

▲

## Chapter 12
## Relationship as a Vehicle for Lessons

*D*iscussions of relationships often have a tendency to deteriorate into an examination of specific problems and suggestions for possible solutions. But before one can adequately explore the true nature of any specific relationship problem, it is helpful to have a picture of what a healthy relationship would look like. In this way, problems can be viewed in a comprehensive perspective. Below is a picture of the ingredients and proportions of a healthy relationship. Refer to it throughout this presentation.

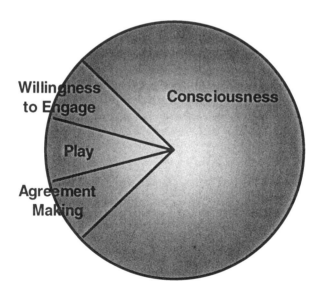

**Picture of a Conscious Relationship**

## The Whole Picture

A relationship is very much a dance. You really do need two to tango. You cannot create a relationship alone. You must have a partner who moves with you to the same tune. You might be able to unilaterally move to the music, but you wouldn't call it a tango. You cannot foretell if you will ever have a dance partner. You cannot make a partner occur when there is none. You can, however, learn to dance, and prepare yourself to be a good partner, should it be part of your path to encounter a partner who wants to dance with you.

If you are in a relationship, making it a healthy relationship involves both partners. Dancing with a *resistant* partner can only be *frustrating, tiring,* and *futile.* You wouldn't want to drag around a non-participating partner in your dance. You could do it, for a while. But even if you dedicated all of your life to this impossible task, you would eventually run out of energy.

Ask yourself, "Why would I want to try to dance with someone who doesn't want to participate? Am I just *afraid* of being *alone*? Am I operating under a belief that my partner will eventually choose to engage in the dance, if I only hang in there long enough?" Feel, explore, claim your truth, and choose truthful behavior. A healthy relationship begins with you claiming your personal truth about such a relationship. A "healthy relationship" means that it is alive. It must be growing, changing and evolving continuously. In order to do this, both partners must be *invested* in nurturing its growth.

Your first conscious choice in regard to a relationship, then, would be a choice to be willing to engage with the other. Typically this early level of engagement is superficial; *hopeful* but not *invested,* a "wait-and-see" attitude. You and your partner would probably participate in some form of play, usually called dating. You might have coffee together one afternoon, and *enjoy* the wit of the conversation. If you feel a stronger sense of *attraction* as a result of this play, you would probably be inclined to make an agreement to see each other again in the near future. Your emotions are strong, and are generally recognized as positive. These emotions offer opportunities to discover a deeper truth, and claim a higher consciousness. But since they are positive, they will probably just be *enjoyed.*

As you make another choice to be willing to engage with this person, you might try other forms of play. Perhaps you would spend the day together *enjoying* an activity. Depending upon your continued sense of *attraction,* you would make new agreements as closure to this day. These might be anything from "I'll call you sometime." to "Yes, I'd *love* to go to dinner and a movie with you next Saturday!" Again, you walk away with emotions which can further your growth in consciousness.

This pattern continues as long as you continue to feel more strongly *attracted* to this person. The relationship is minimal at first, but it progresses more deeply in each of the four areas of relating: engaging, playing, agreement making, and realizing consciousness. The emotions you feel about the relationship are *intense.* Your emotions may be very *intense*, even to the degree that you declare them as *"love."* But the relationship itself is still minimal at this early stage of development. Each renewal of the relationship, a completion of all four parts, requires another choice to engage further. The relationship grows. An expanding spiral represents the progress of the growth.

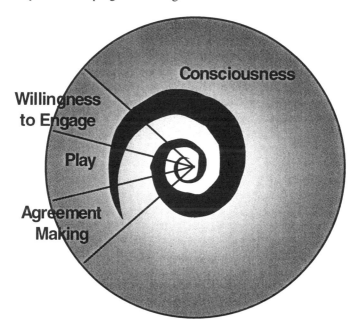

**Growth in a Relationship**

Pursuit of higher consciousness, by both partners, creates three-fourths of a healthy relationship. The remaining one-fourth is the actual "relating" to one another. With each completion of a growth cycle, you must make a new choice to be willing to engage at a deeper level. You play at more significant levels. You make more meaningful agreements. All of which then presents you with another set of emotions, from which you can claim more of your personal truth. In this way you use the relationship to discover more of your truth, and claim higher consciousness.

Many relationship seminars, marriage seminars, books, videotapes, audiotapes, TV shows, etc., focus on the skills involved in the "relating" to each other. While these skills are important, in sum they represent only 25% of the relationship. No matter how many relationship skills, communication skills, sex skills, or problem solving skills you acquire, you will be attending to only one-fourth of the whole relationship. Without an individual focus on the pursuit of higher consciousness, there cannot be a healthy relationship.

Conversely, while consciousness is the lion's share of a healthy relationship, fully 75%, you still cannot achieve a conscious relationship without the remaining 25% of relating skills. You cannot have a conscious relationship without proportionate focus in all four areas; three in relating to others, constituting 25% of the relationship, and one in consciousness, totaling 75% of the conscious relationship.

**Willingness to Engage**

"Willingness to engage", the beginning of any relationship, refers to the spectrum of behaviors possible to experience with another human. Assuming that behavior toward another is somewhat associated with the degree of *intimacy* you feel, everything from saying "hello" to a passerby, to full willingness to participate in the resolution of a partner's issues, fits on this spectrum. At each stage of development you must make another choice about your willingness to engage. With most people, you will reach a limit to your willingness, and curtail any further development of the relationship.

The spectrum of willingness to engage includes these behaviors, as examples: (Extreme unwillingness to engage might be pathologic, such as in agoraphobia, or it might be a choice made in the pursuit of some other desire, such as a recluse or hermit.)

- You choose to go out into the world, where other

people exist, such as going to a lecture or a social gathering.

- You might respond to someone else's contact with you (e.g. answering the telephone).
- You can initiate a contact with someone else (e.g. stopping someone in a store for a polite, superficial conversation).
- You can converse with someone for a lengthy period of time, requiring a stretching for greater depth of conversation.
- You could meet for lunch, or to have a cup of tea together.
- You might spend an afternoon engaged in a shared activity, such as bike riding or hiking.
- You decide to spend an evening together at a more intimate activity, such as dinner or dancing.
- One of you offers to cook a meal for the other and share it together in the more private location of a home.
- You decide to share more personal information with each other, such as your history, your dreams, and your goals.
- You spend an evening with the other person along with their children.
- You share some intimate information about you, like your *fears*, your *desires*, etc.
- You decide to be more physically demonstrative of your attraction. You kiss, hold hands, wrap an arm around, etc.
- You spend a weekend together, away from your normal routine.
- You process a minor *annoyance* about each other.
- You increase the level of sexual contact.
- You begin to speak of a future together.
- You share a relationship "wish list" and discuss how to blend your two pictures.
- You mutually decide that you will begin to create this shared picture. This may be engagement to marriage, co-habitation, or some other form of commitment to each other.

- You work through a power struggle, and create some specific agreements about how you will behave with each other. You repeat this step, many times.
- You expose things about yourself that you thought you would never say to anyone.
- You show *respect* for the issues that your partner is sharing with you.
- You purposely strive to create an environment of *safety* for your partner.
- You share with your partner what you *need* from him or her in order to invite your *safety.*
- You find new insights into who you are, each time you expose new levels of *vulnerability* with your partner.
- Your power struggles become less frequent and less intense when you feel issues arising. Rather than blame the other person for your *discomfort*, you both strive to claim higher consciousness.
- Your relationship becomes more and more the focus of your life, as it provides you your "growth point."
- You experience the inner power derived from core issues as a direct result of the *unconditional love* you experience from your partner. You commit to new levels of relating with each other.
- You agree to keep a watchful eye for any of your partner's issues, now that you know them as well as he or she does. You become full partners in the dealing with two sets of core issues. Your own pace of growth escalates dramatically. You can see in each other the growth steps made in coming to higher consciousness.
- Your relationship becomes a "gift" you can share with others, by modeling, teaching, sharing: finding new depths of *vulnerability* to explore in yourself with your partner.
- (The spectrum continues through all levels of consciousness.)

You may choose to limit your willingness to engage anywhere on the spectrum for any number of reasons, some of which are healthy, and some of which are not. When you feel as though your willingness to engage is *approaching a limit*, it is important to again use the Path of Emotion to feel, explore, claim your truth, and choose truthful behavior. Don't assume that just because you feel you *reached your limit*, it is truthful to cease the relationship. You may feel your *willingness is limited*, only to find upon exploration, it does not meet the ring of truth. Terminating your involvement, when you first experience *limited willingness*, may be an unconscious reaction, rather than a conscious choice.

Similarly, you may be *ambivalent* about your willingness to engage. *Willingness* may increase and decrease, depending upon various factors. Feeling *limited willingness* may not be a long-term experience, but only a temporary reaction to your own issues. Explore your emotions, including the limits of your willingness to engage. This may be how your next lessons are emerging. After re-committing to your own growth, you might choose to expand your willingness.

It is always healthy to limit your engagement when you accurately perceive an imminent *danger* to you or someone for whom you have responsibility. Your willingness to engage with someone should be limited when you see that to continue engaging might bring physical harm to you. However, even then, engagement could be healthy, but only if it is in accordance with your personal truth to do so.

If you think it is truthful for you to allow yourself to be violated through physical abuse, sexual abuse, emotional abuse, mental abuse, or spiritual abuse, you need to check out this belief for its validity, very carefully and thoroughly. You would want to use a professional counselor to make sure you are using the skills appropriately. It is not likely that suffering acts of violence in a personal relationship is ever truthful. It is a general rule that what is healthy is truthful, and what is truthful is healthy. Rare exceptions may exist, but they should be viewed with much skepticism.

"Healthy" is defined according to how you arrive at your choice of behavior. If you choose behavior so that you are acting in accordance with your personal truth, you will always be behaving in a healthy manner, even if you die. BEing in truth is the highest form of health, although it is not always greeted with *enthusiasm* from those around you. You may act in complete accordance with your personal truth, and suffer the consequence of violent reaction from others. Healthiness of behavior cannot be determined by the consequences of your action. Healthiness must be measured by the process you use to make your choice.

What is deemed healthy by 99.9% of the population may not

necessarily be healthy for you, in any given moment. Only you can decide what behavior is in accordance with your truth. Likewise, what is considered by most of the world to be unhealthy, may indeed be in accordance with your truth, and therefore healthy for you. The behavior is healthy if it brings you greater self-awareness, allows you to connect with and to deal with your issues, and leads you to a higher level of consciousness. Your inner measure is the only measure that counts. Some of the healthiest individuals known to man have been shot, burned, crucified, imprisoned, or otherwise rejected from the people around them. You are the only person who can assess your personal truth. BEing in truth is the most courageous path anyone can walk.

Limiting your willingness to engage with someone may therefore either be healthy or unhealthy. As a general rule, you will probably limit your engagement when you no longer feel *attraction* to him or her. But you must first explore these emotions. Upon determining it is your truth to cease engaging, then behave accordingly. If you feel *attraction*, but you experience *frustration, dismay, anger,* or *fear,* etc., then it would not be a healthy behavior to limit your engagement; at least not until after you have dealt with those experiences.

Many relationships get stuck, or even end, when repeated arguments bring up *uncomfortable* emotions in one or both people. You will always experience an *inclination to withdraw* from the other person when this happens. It is an unconscious survival mechanism to withdraw from *pain.* Instead of withdrawing, however, this is exactly when you need to explore your willingness to engage, in relation to your *uncomfortable* emotions. Use the emotions you are feeling to further the connection to the other person, by working through them together. Your willingness to engage does not need to be limited just because you are feeling *uncomfortable* emotions.

A healthy person will choose to not be the limiting factor to any relationship that is based in truth. Let every relationship develop to the limits of your *attraction* and the depths of truth it presents, both of which change and mature as you feel *appreciation* for their presence in your life. Barring premature limits, let the other person set the limits to engagement. In this way, you can participate in every relationship for your greatest growth. Of course this is a general message about healthy behavior. As stated above, only you, in your personal truth, can determine what is healthy in the moment.

## Play

"Play" is the way in which you *enjoy* the company of another in a shared activity. Since it involves an emotional experience, it is impossible to absolutely define any activity as play. As in "willingness to engage," there is a spectrum of activities that might fit this definition, but the spectrum will be very individualized. Your spectrum of play will be very different than someone else's spectrum of play.

When you first come in contact with someone that you are *attracted* to, it may be *playful* to merely be in the same room, or perhaps to pass each other and smile. The list might include:

- Having a short conversation
- Planning to do something together
- Sharing food or drink
- Exchanging gifts
- Verbal or written communication about feelings
- Introducing the other to an interest of yours
- Learning about each other's history
- *Enjoying* a piece of entertainment together
- Including the other person in your world
- Making plans to maintain a connection
- Discovering a place or an activity or an idea together
- Sharing your awareness about yourself with each other
- Giving feedback to the other person about something you don't *like*
- Hearing, with *appreciation,* feedback from them about something they don't *like* in you
- Mutual involvement in the resolution of a problem between you
- Commitment to always BEing There for the shared purpose of resolving individual issues
- These are but some of the behaviors that can comprise the spectrum of play in a relationship.

Of course, physical contact must be integrated into this spectrum. Here are some of the physical contacts that make up "play" in a relationship:

- The "accidental" brushing in the hallway
- Making a deliberate touch with your hand

- A *friendly* embrace
- Holding hands
- A "non-sexual" kiss on the cheek
- Dancing together
- Mutual massage
- Sexual foreplay
- The more deliberate sexual acts of petting, kissing, fellatio, cunnilingus, and intercourse
- Experimenting together with sexual *prejudices*
- Using sex to deliberately pursue greater consciousness, by choosing deeper *vulnerability*
- Expanding your sexual practices to include greater variety and mutual discovery
- Learning to fully appreciate your partner's experience of *pleasure*
- *Enjoying* the discoveries made through sexual yoga

Each of these invites a whole new emotional set, which can either add to, or detract from, your sense of *attraction*. The escalation of play in a healthy relationship must be in accordance with your truth, which implies that you are making conscious choices to engage at increasingly more meaningful levels, and claiming full responsibility for your behavior, your emotions, and your personal truth with each choice.

**Agreement Making**

"Agreements" in a healthy relationship deal with the questions that arise naturally between two people who are attracted to each other, but don't yet know how best to BE together for their mutual growth. Beginning a new relationship can take you into a wide variety of uncommon emotions, some *frightening* and some fraught with *extreme expectation*. Just as if you won a million dollar lottery, you would probably *anticipate* its delivery, and *worry* about how it might affect your life. With the significant change of a new relationship, questions arise naturally: questions about when to *expect* certain experiences, questions about the affect of those experiences, questions about future *pain* and *security*, questions about predicting future behavior. Agreements are a way of using these organic questions to cure the bonds that are developing. Before the test of time and the benefit of history, agreements with your new partner help to establish a common reality. They help to apply the energy inherent in *fears of the unknown* into the creation of a somewhat *predictable* and *reliable* future.

Agreements must be mutual and they must be verbalized, at all levels of engagement, and at all levels of commitment. Agreements can be very simple at first, such as an agreement to "get together sometime." But with every rotation through the elements of the healthy relationship, the agreements become more complex. The agreement, "I'll call you," can be interpreted in different ways. Make agreements as specific and detailed as possible and practical. The "romantic mystery" associated with the question, "Will he or won't he," is very short-lived. Does "I'll call you" mean "Don't wait around for me" or does it mean "I expect you to answer whenever I do call" or does it mean "I don't want to get further involved with you" or does it mean "as soon as I get home?" A healthy relationship involves speaking your truth, speaking truthfully, and doing everything possible to invite the other person to do the same.

Questions leading to more complex agreements include:

- Should we spend more and more time together?
- How do we consider the other person's *needs* and *desires* when making plans?
- What will be the focus of your time together?
- When and how should we include sex in the relationship?
- Should we be monogamous with each other?
- When should we co-habitate?
- What meaning does marriage have for each of us?
- What level of honesty do we ask and expect from each other?
- What will be our roles in solving problems between us?
- How will we assist each other in resolving inner issues?
- What are the expectations of including previous friends in this relationship?

And the list goes on infinitely.

Of course, making agreements requires discussion of each person's experience, a mutual exploration. Discussing the natural questions of a healthy relationship involves *openness* about the questions you have, *vulnerability* in sharing your *fears* and *desires*, *sensitivity* to the other person's *vulnerability*, and a *desire* for a mutual agreement.

The antithesis of agreement making is to make assumptions instead. Assumptions are easy to make, hard to break, and almost always lead, eventually, to well-intended hassles. Problems between partners in a relationship can often be avoided if you minimize the assumptions you make about your partner's behavior and emotions. Check things out by asking questions, even at the risk of looking *stupid*, or receiving an unpleasant reaction. Then make mutual agreements. This simple step in a relationship will save infinite trouble. Make it an agreement in your relationship to not make assumptions. Or, at the very least, make agreements about what assumptions are okay to make. Unilateral agreements are not agreements.

Unspoken agreements are not agreements. Agreements can never be assumed, at least not until there is a high degree of mutual familiarity. Even then, it is potentially hazardous to your compatibility to assume an agreement exists when it has not been thoroughly discussed and mutually agreed. No one *wants* to be held to a contract they did not sign, even if they have no *objections* to the content of the contract. As you get to know each other well, you can discuss what things are okay to make assumptions about. This becomes one of your agreements.

What many people consider the ultimate relationship commitment, marriage, is in its base definition, a set of agreements. It is the agreements in marriage that help establish it as a unique relationship and a divine event. Unfortunately, most marriages begin with assumed agreements, made unconsciously, and based in individual issues. Given such a beginning, is it any wonder that most marriages end in divorce? Without consciousness, marriage is not given the opportunity to develop into the vehicle for personal growth into higher consciousness that it is divinely meant to be. Agreements, such as these below, are all agreements that would be part of the vows of a conscious marriage:

- "We acknowledge the other person as our negative image, our counterpart, and we find our wholeness in our mutual endeavor."
- "We are going to both invest in a bonded relationship that will supercede all others, except my relationship with myself, my truth, and my God."
- "Marriage means we bring everything home to be mutually shared."
- "Your issues will be as high a priority to me as my issues."
- "We mutually agree to create *trust* and *reliability* so that you may experience your issues in a *safe* environment, and we will make further agreements

about specific behavior that assists this agreement."

- "We will hold sacred each others core issues, recognizing that they are the points of greatest vulnerability, and therefore have the greatest potential for personal growth into higher consciousness. Being sacred, we will not treat them *carelessly* or *maliciously.*"
- "We are endeavoring together to create an emotional experience of *intimacy*, and possibly *unity.*"
- "We will not abandon this divine vehicle until all the issues that separate us have been thoroughly explored, in truth, and we have both arrived at a truth that necessitates our separation."

It is almost impossible to imagine that a relationship based in such profound truth, with such powerful agreements, would ever dissolve, not because of the specific agreements, but because of the process required to create them.

When you can picture the growth cycle of a healthy relationship, you can make new and clearer agreements in your marriage, continuously, with each piece of added consciousness. A relationship must grow, and growth means change. The change is good and healthy. The relationship must grow if it is to survive. It is either growing, or it is dying. There is no in-between, no status quo. New and deeper agreements, on a continuous basis, indicate which direction it takes.

Do not make agreements that you are not ready to keep. Do not make agreements that are not truthful for you. If you choose to make an agreement in which you are not claiming full responsibility for your behavior, or one that you are not fully prepared to uphold, you will either sabotage the agreement or create *resentment* toward your partner or yourself. This leads to an undermining and diminishment of *trust* in your relationship. An agreement is a behavior. Your behavior is always your responsibility. Be fully conscious, and fully responsible, when making agreements. Many people base their *trust* on your word. If you give your word, you are saying that you are trustworthy. If you wish to remain being seen as trustworthy, you need to be very deliberate about giving your word in the form of an agreement. If you are not ready to make an agreement, engage in more thorough mutual exploration. A mutually shared truth about an issue is the only truth that both partners can truthfully uphold.

**Stages of Romance-based Relationships**

Now that you know the elements of a healthy relationship, and are familiar with its growth pattern, it is important to also be familiar with the stages of a relationship. The best reference for this information is a book by Harville Hendrix, titled Getting The Love You Want - A Guide For Couples (Henry Holt & Company, New York, @1988.) In his book, Hendrix describes the three universal stages of a romantic relationship, and a fourth stage available to those who are willing to do the work.

The first three stages of every romantic relationship are the attraction stage, the romance stage, and the power struggle stage. Romantic *attraction* is created when you come into contact with someone who matches a pre-determined set of criteria that exists within your own unconscious. This set of criteria, called your Imago, is created through the imprinting that occurs during your childhood, primarily by your caretakers.

Imagine if your caretakers, including your mother and father, or step-parents, nanny, grandparents, aunts, uncles, brothers, sisters, daycare persons, etc., whomever was responsible for your survival during your early years, could be gathered together close to a wall, and a bright light was flashed on them. Your Imago would be the silhouette that was cast of all your primary caretakers, those people responsible for your survival. Imago includes all of the good and bad characteristics of these primary caretakers, with special emphasis on the bad, as it is the life-threatening experiences that create the deeper imprints. (See Chapter 2, **The Unconscious**) This silhouette creates a type of template, which acts as a screening device for all the people you ever come across in your life.

As you encounter people in your adult life, you will feel *attraction* to those who match your Imago. If you choose to engage with this person, your sense of attraction will either increase or decrease, depending upon how closely they match your Imago. The closer the match, the stronger the *attraction* will be. If, as you get to know this person, you discover they are not closely matched to your Imago, then you will experience a decreased sense of *attraction*.

Despite all the things you say to yourself about why you are attracted to someone, "they are the right size," or "they look the right way," or "they do the right things," etc., your real *interest* in someone comes out of a more profound place within you. While all the observations you make about someone may indeed *stimulate* your *interest* in them, what you find *interesting* was established long before you were in control of your unconscious. Hendrix gives an excellent description of how this happens, and what it means to you in your adult relationships. We *enthusiastically* refer you to his writings.

The next stage, after feeling *attraction,* is called the romance stage. It is here that your sense of *attraction* is tested. It is also here that your unconscious tries to "win over" the person it believes is going to enhance, and perhaps even guarantee, your survival. So it helps you to "put on your best face." During this stage, you typically feel very *energetic,* and you show few *needs.* Your primary tactic in trying to win their affection and commitment is to imply that you will fulfill their deepest needs. "You'll always be there." "You'll never leave." "You'll always take care of them." "You'll always be happy together." And so on.

Your partner, reacting to his or her Imago, is also doing the same unconscious dynamics. You each encounter the best of each other. Life feels *good* during the romance stage of relationships, but you cannot create true *intimacy* in this stage. The romance stage lasts as long as your sense of *attraction* continues. As you cycle through many phases of relationship, you will *need to make agreements* with each other, some of which will speak to your level of *commitment.* Commitments are made to *assure* each other that your promises for fulfillment will be honored, even at those times when you are not in touch with your *attraction.*

When you make commitments to each other, the third stage of a relationship begins: the power struggle. Your unconscious *expects* a payoff for all the superhuman effort put forth in the romance stage. It wants *fulfillment* of the promises made to make you *whole* and *right.* Your unconscious *expects* your partner to give you what was promised during the romance stage: wholeness. Since your partner was unaware of the unspoken expectations of your unconscious, the healing isn't forthcoming. Unconsciously, you perceive this as withholding, perhaps even *malicious* withholding, and you are *puzzled* by this apparent desire to *hurt* you further. Your unconscious sends you the emotional messages to *beware,* that things aren't what they were supposed to be.

To complicate the dynamics even more, the same thing is happening within your partner. Both of you are not getting what you believed was promised you. You perceive your partner as a perpetrator of the *hurt* that already existed within your unconscious, as imprinting. Your partner has unconsciously become the bad guy.

You both negotiate getting your needs met, not a nice clean verbalized negotiation, but a negotiation of behaviors. One tactic is to close down, hold your cards more closely, and adopt an attitude of giving if and when you receive. It is subtle, usually. It is unconscious. And it is *puzzling*. What started out looking like the answer to your prayers, as what you were always looking for, slowly turns into a daily struggle for who is going to get their needs met first.

The power struggle is where most married couples get stuck. It can last for the lifetime of the marriage, ended only through death or by terminating the marriage. Often, one or both partners begin to look outside the marriage to get their *needs* met, whether it is a need for compatible sex, mental stimulation, companionship, or just plain *acceptance*. They develop "parallel relationships." This can take the form of an extra-marital affair, or a focus on work or home or children, getting actively involved in community or church affairs, or taking up a recreational activity that requires much time. There are many other ways to successfully avoid the on-going *hurt* and *disappointment* of a romantic relationship that is in the power struggle stage.

Those who terminate their marriage in an effort to deal with this *hurt* and *disappointment* will inevitably start the cycle over again in a new romantic relationship: attraction, romance, and power struggle. And again, they are confronted with the dilemma of living with the *pain* or ending the relationship.

While these stages of relationship may sound very *hopeless* and pointless, Hendrix also describes how there is a divine perfection at work in this process. It is neither pointless nor *hopeless*. The point of allowing this inherent process to unfold is to create an environment where you can begin to deal with your core issues. In order to do this, it is first necessary to re-create an environment similar to the one where the imprinting first occurred. This brings you face-to-face with your *existential pain*, the underlying motivation for your search for meaning and purpose in your life. Falling in *love* with your Imago match is the vehicle for bringing you this opportunity.

The *hope* lies in discovering that there is a method for transcending the power struggle and developing a romantic relationship to a fourth stage, called the conscious relationship. A conscious relationship begins with the pursuit of higher consciousness, an individual endeavor. This is the beginning of the healthy relationship. It starts with a total commitment to your own consciousness growth.

If you hold such a commitment, then one of the early agreements you will seek in a developing relationship will be a similar commitment in your partner. You know that a relationship will lead to an experience of intimacy only if both partners are seeking their higher consciousness. It is only in this way that there can be a deep *respect* from your partner for the consciousness you seek. Together, you make an agreement to use the relationship as a vehicle for the pursuit of consciousness, for both individuals.

To fully understand how a relationship serves as a vehicle for encountering the lessons needed for your growth in consciousness, it is important to understand that your lessons have been determined, or at least defined, by the experiences of your childhood. If you believe in the spiritual principle of reincarnation, then there is the additional piece of understanding that your lessons were determined in your spirit form, before you incarnated through your parents. But even without this spiritual belief, it is not difficult to see how your lessons were given earthly definition through the experiences you had as an infant and young child. (See Part I: **The Foundation**)

The ways in which you were imprinted defined how you see the world, how you translate specific experiences, how you perceive the behaviors of others, what you take on as purpose in your BEing; in short, your reality. You cannot take on the real work of consciousness growth, or creating a conscious relationship, until you have some degree of self-awareness about the reality from which you are beginning.

This self-awareness about your fundamental reality can be pursued in many different ways. The most efficient way is to use the Path of Emotion to <u>feel your way along</u>. When you are exploring your emotions, track them back to ever-deeper levels of experience. Continue the exploration as far as you can go with every emotional path. With practice you will discover your core issues at the root of every experience.

Your core issues define your lessons. And your growth into higher consciousness is dependent upon learning these lessons. Your core lessons are different representations of one simple human lesson. The human lesson is always the same: claim higher levels of self-responsibility, as exhibited in you claiming your up-to-date personal truth and choosing behavior that is consistent with your personal truth.

It is in this light that you must pursue knowledge about the experiences of your childhood, especially those that might have had an impact upon your survival. To pursue full understanding of your childhood allows you to be fully present in your adulthood. It is not with an attitude of finding fault or laying *blame* that you pursue the information of your childhood imprints. It is not necessary to accuse anyone. Nor is it necessary to relieve anyone's *guilt, shame,* or sense of *inadequacy.* All of these purposes would betray your intent to claim, and limit, your self-responsibility.

Likewise, neither is *forgiveness* your intent. *Forgiveness* is a highly touted moral teaching that went along with the perception that you could control what you felt, as though *forgiving* someone meant you should no longer feel what you feel. In order to feel *virtuous,* you were taught that is was necessary to rid yourself of emotions that supposedly interfered with *virtue.* It was an exercise in denial.

Now that you understand that there are no "bad" emotions, and that many seemingly contradictory emotions can exist in a single complex emotional tapestry, you can put all emotional energy to constructive use by using it to realize higher levels of consciousness. The emotional *struggle* of striving for *forgiveness* is irrelevant.

*Forgiveness* is possible for any situation in your life, but only if certain events transpire. The ingredients necessary for you to be able to *forgive* someone in truth, that is, have the offense be a completed experience for you, are: Acknowledgment; Responsibility; and Commitment.

Acknowledgment means that the offending person shows an understanding and *appreciation* for your experience. They empathize with you and validate your emotional experience.

Second, they need to claim full responsibility for their behavior, and owning that their behavior had a significant impact upon you.

And third, they make a commitment to change their behavior, so as to never create that experience again, and a commitment to assist you in your process of integration of that experience, wherever and whenever possible.

When an offender can make these presentations in truth, then it is possible for you to complete the trauma by *realizing* the divinity in all experience. You arrive at a *profound understanding* that even the most *horrible* experiences can be *appreciated* for the opportunities they present. When this occurs, there is a *deeply experienced sense of appreciation* for the lessons inherent in the experience. This *appreciation,* in turn, transforms the *pain.* It dissipates the *horror.* And *forgiveness* occurs.

But before these things occur, *forgiveness* is moot. It amounts to an exercise in denial. You would be far more effective to explore your *troubling* emotions of *anger, injustice, terror, hurt,* etc., and discover the "emotional juice" to be used to claim more of your truth.

*Forgiveness* is an act of relationship that requires willingness to engage at a far deeper level than that which was possible when denial was prevalent. But it is not possible until the necessary ingredients are present. *Forgiveness* occurs as a result of resolving the problem between you and the person whom you feel has *wronged you*, not just because you want it to. If the problems are resolved, then *forgiveness* occurs naturally as you gain *appreciation* for the lessons learned. If the problems are not resolved, then *forgiveness* is not possible and the choice to engage further in the relationship is of questionable value.

What kind of relationship are you engaging in if your partner refuses his or her responsibility for their behavior, or refuses to process together until a resolution is created? It certainly would not be a relationship based upon the mutual pursuit of *intimacy*, which lies at the heart of all romantic relationships, and possibly at the heart of all human interaction. The inherent need for *intimacy* is the emotional drive of romance. The need for *intimacy* is the pursuit of *wholeness*, of becoming masters of our consciousness. The conscious relationship recognizes the divine perfection in a romantic relationship that develops to the power struggle, and then through the mutual effort of both partners to create *intimacy*, provides an environment and a means for them to seek self-awareness and higher consciousness.

To pursue *intimacy* is to strive to learn how to *unite* with at least one other person. *Uniting* with one person then makes it possible to learn how to *unite* with all people, then with all things, and then with God. The pursuit of *intimacy* is nothing short of the pursuit of God. Romantic relationships are the vehicle by which you seek God. Romantic relationships are indeed, the holiest of all holy work. And it all unfolds through the pursuit of *intimacy*.

*Intimacy* is as fundamental a need on the emotional aspect as water is on the physical aspect. You can survive without *intimacy* for a short while. But, by going without it too long, you will die. *Intimacy* is a *basic need*, an *urge*, a *must,* a *compulsion*. *Intimacy* is what you are pursuing in your romantic relationships. It is the ambrosia for what ails you. It is the *soulful peace* that you *long* for. It is the feeling of *having arrived*, of BEing There.

For most people however, *intimacy* is a very elusive experience. Bits and pieces of *intimacy* are regarded as *coveted* treasures; so much so, that otherwise intelligent people will surrender nearly all of their truth to keep small pieces of it. For *fear* of losing the memory of an *intimate* moment, as though it was a thing that could be possessed, they will remain locked in a never-ending power struggle.

*Intimacy* is not a thing. And sustained *intimacy* does not happen accidentally. It is an emotion. And all emotions occur for specific reasons. All emotions arise from your beliefs, your values, your perceptions, and your early life experience. As you learn and practice the Path of Emotion, you increase your ability to create what you truly want. What you truly want includes *intimacy*. As you practice the Path of Emotion, you claim more consciousness. Practicing the pursuit of consciousness, as a foundation process even before *concerning* yourself with relationships, you are prepared to exercise that consciousness in relating to others. When you relate to others consciously, beyond the power struggle, you begin to experience moments of *intimacy*. The more you practice relating in truth, by BEing conscious, the more frequently you experience the moments of *intimacy*.

A conscious relationship is an on-going process of relating in truth. A relationship is more action than thing; it should be stated as a verb, instead of a noun. Instead of a "relationship," it should be a "relating." Relating is a process. It is the process of doing and improving the other three areas of a conscious relationship: willingness to engage, play, and agreements. Relating with consciousness is the spiraling through the four areas of a healthy relationship at progressively deeper levels in each area. It means literally feeling your way along in an effort to create *intimacy*.

---

## INTIMACY <= SAFETY + VULNERABILITY

---

The creation of *intimacy* requires the presence of two very specific experiences that precede it, both of which can be intentionally developed: *safety* and *vulnerability*. By learning the skills necessary to create the emotions of *safety* and *vulnerability*, you will be learning to create *intimacy*. Neither of these skills is more important than the other. They both must be attended to frequently. And they must be in proportion to each other. There is no *intimacy* when you are *vulnerable* in the absence of *safety*. Nor is there *intimacy* when you are *safe* in the absence of *vulnerability*. Both are necessary for the creation of *intimacy*.

---

## INTIMACY <= SAFETY + VULNERABILITY

---

*Safety* is an emotional experience, and therefore it is your creation and your responsibility. *Safety* is the experience of *trusting* the other humans in your environment, that they will *accept* you, right as you are, right in this moment, and that they will never behave in any way that would purposely invite your *pain* or *discomfort*. This does not mean they might not inadvertently behave in a way that invites your *discomfort*. As imperfect human beings, it would be *unfair* to *expect* behavior that never challenged your creation of *safety*. *Trust* of someone does mean they are committed to never doing so with *malicious intent*.

Some of the qualities about others that are frequently listed as being helpful in the creation of *safety* are:

- Display of *empathy:* That is, the other person shows to you that they can understand and *respect* the emotional experiences that you are describing, without *judging* you for what you are feeling.
- Ability to keep a confidence, meaning they are *concerned* about what information of yours is private, and they maintain that privacy.
- The other person shows a *willingness* to engage with you in meaningful emotional dialog, which is merely an indicator of their *willingness* to feel and to deal with their own emotions.
- A displayed *desire* to relate to your experiences through experiences of their own, a sign of their *willingness* to be *vulnerable* with you.

In the development of *intimacy, safety* must be the first concern and *vulnerability* the second. As you will see later in problem resolution, the dynamics of an interaction will determine the outcome of the conflict. Until you are an advanced seeker of higher consciousness, dynamics must be attended to first, and content second. In the development of *intimacy*, creation of *safety* requires attending to the dynamics, and *vulnerability* involves the content of experiences.

Safety involves two phases: inviting a feeling of *safety* in others, and feeling *safe* from the acts of others. You can develop your ability to invite *safety* in others by exercising those qualities listed above: empathy, confidentiality, willingness to engage, and *vulnerability*. You can practice these skills with anyone, anywhere, anytime, with or without their knowledge. By being *safe,* you invite others to share their *vulnerability* with you. Even before engaging in a conscious relationship, by being *safe* you create more of a sense of *connection* with your world, and consequently, more *intimacy*.

In measuring the level of *safety* you feel in engaging with another, follow the Path of Emotion. Tune-in to what you feel. If you feel *doubt*, or *suspicion*, or *fear*, etc., then explore it with the other person. (e.g. "I have *fears* about your safety. Can you help me understand them?") In this communication you have claimed full responsibility for your emotion, and you have chosen to act on them by engaging at a meaningful level with the other person.

That person's *willingness* to engage with you will be the first indicator of their safety. If they respond, "Sure, I'll help you explore your fears about my safety", then you have already made the first step in alleviating your *fear*. If they refuse to engage with you, if they take *offense* at your honesty, if they react *defensively* and blame or criticize, then you have *validated* your first experience of *fear*, by confirming that they display unsafe dynamics. *Safety* will be the first issue you must deal with in order to create *intimacy* with that person.

There is a self-defeating trap in measuring your *safety* while engaged with others. If in measuring *safety,* you easily dismiss others as *not safe*, you will never get to a place in relationships where you can create *intimacy*. The trap leads you to believe that no one is *safe enough* to engage with. Instead, you must remind yourself that the *safety* you feel is your emotion, and therefore your creation. The other person is not responsible for the *safety* you feel or don't feel. Determining that they are *not safe* does not mean that you will never experience them as *safe*. Use that relationship, and every relationship, as a vehicle for you to discover and claim a deeper personal truth. Perhaps you can learn to create the experience of *safety* more easily. Perhaps it is one of your issues that you cannot easily create the experience of *safety*.

In developing a relationship of *intimacy,* there are specific things you can do to help invite and create *safety*. First, learn to listen to the other person, actively listen. This involves behavior that is much more than passively receiving information. Active listening involves a *desire* to understand what the other person is saying with their words, and even more, what they are meaning underneath their words.

In every communication there are two roles, the sender and the receiver. It requires the active participation of both parts in order to have a successful communication. The sender is trying to convey thoughts and feelings by using words, gestures, expressions, postures, etc. They have a picture in their mind that they want to share with you. The picture may or may not be clear to them as they attempt to send it.

You, as a receiver, can help the sender communicate by telling them what you are receiving. You feed back the picture you receive to the sender by paraphrasing what you are hearing from them. This gives the sender a chance to confirm what you have received, or to change the message so that it is closer to what it is they are trying to send. Paraphrasing may be the single most important skill involved in active listening.

Beyond this, you can ask questions about the meaning of someone's communication. You can relate their feelings to specific situations. You can try to simplify, generalize, or *identify* with the feelings of the sender. These are all communication skills that you can develop in an effort to help create *safety* in you, and invite in others. By far however, the most important communication skill, in assuring an accurate message, is to paraphrase what you are receiving back to the sender so they can own it or modify it.

Actively listening to someone's communication tells that person that you prioritize the relationship. You convey to them that you want to create *intimacy* above all else, except your own health and pursuit of consciousness. If you know that the relationship is more important to your partner than their work, their golf or tennis dates, their business contacts, newspaper, TV shows, chores, sleep, etc., then you will probably be invited to feel very *important*. Feeling *important* is a powerful pre-cursor to inviting *safety*. You, in turn, can invite this same experience in your partner by prioritizing your relationship above all else.

Prioritizing a relationship is not the same as depending upon it or merely striving to keep it. Trying to keep a relationship, usually invites you to move further away from your personal truth. "Keeping" implies an attempt to possess it, to nail it down. A relationship must live freely in order to grow healthy. As soon as you begin to constrict the relationship, or your own truth, then any changes that follow will be a movement toward its demise, and eventual death.

Your higher priorities, however, must be to your own health and growth. This will ensure that any energy you put into a relationship will be behavior that reflects your personal truth. If anything other than your health and growth, such as your attachment to a relationship, is prioritized above the freely growing healthy relationship, then you are allowing yourself to be diverted from the pursuit of *intimacy*. What could possibly be more important than the pursuit of *intimacy*?

You might answer that your children are more important than a romantic relationship. But how so? You can never have a fully realized, intimate relationship with your children, at least not until they are fully responsible adults. You can invite *safety* and *vulnerability* in your children, and therefore invite them to feel *intimate* with you as a parent. And you might feel *safe* with your child. But you can never create *vulnerability* in yourself with them. As a young child, they do not have the capacity to relate with you at your level of experience. So you are never fully *vulnerable,* no matter how disclosing you might be. And if you try to share adult experiences with a child who is incapable of relating, whose needs are you really addressing, and how *safe* are you being for them? Are you teaching them to create the experience of *safety* around people who are selfish and self-centered? If so, what kind or relationships are you teaching them to create in their lives?

You can create intimate relationships with your adult children, in so far as you share your experiences with each other. But since incest is universally recognized as a destructive force, you can never include this part of your physical aspect with your child. Being sexual with someone within the context of an intimate relationship opens you to levels of *vulnerability* not possible anywhere else. You cannot pursue sexual intimacy with your children. Therefore, intimate relationships with your children will always have a limit to the depth of *intimacy.* These relationships can be very *close,* very *intimate,* and very *important.* But they can never offer you the same opportunity for attainment of higher consciousness as can a romantic relationship. Whether young or adult, the creation of *intimacy* with your children is limited. Parenting children with *love* is essential to their health and growth. But it is clear that children cannot be put into a position of priority higher than your pursuit of intimacy in a primary romantic relationship.

The third thing you can do to help create *safety* in your relationship, in addition to practicing the communication skills of active listening and paraphrasing, is to make an agreement with your partner to be completely honest with each other. This not only means being honest from this point forward, but it also means that you will "come clean" with everything with each other.

You cannot keep secrets and create *intimacy.* No quibbling. No exceptions. Secrets and *intimacy* are antithetical to each other. There is no such thing as "just going on from here." You carry your past with you in many different ways. The past is always affecting the present. If it is not an integrated past, one in which you effectively use the emotional energy to update and claim your personal truth and use to guide your current choices in behavior, then you cannot freely create the present.

This presents perhaps, the biggest stumbling block for most people in creating *intimacy*. Everyone feels there is some behavior they did, or some feeling they had, that they would *rather* no one knew about. This is part of the "illusion of separateness" that Ken Keyes refers to in his Twelve Pathways[15]. When we do not *accept* ourselves, we create a belief that no one else will *accept* us either. Similarly, when we do not *love* ourselves, we create a belief that we are *unlovable*. The Biblical commandment "Love others as you love yourself" should more correctly state, "you can *love* others only as much as you *love* yourself." Learning to *love* yourself is what creates the capacity for *loving* others.

Anything that is keeping you from *loving* yourself fully is exactly what needs to be felt, explored, claimed, and used consciously in behavior. Keeping no secrets from your partner involves a process of learning to *love* yourself. Most people report a *tremendous relief* of a heavy burden when they finally disclose their secrets, regardless of their partner's reactions. If your partner *rejects* you, for knowing you more fully, then you have still created a new level of *self-acceptance* and *love* within yourself. You expose your vulnerabilities so that you can more directly deal with those parts of you that are limiting your growth and preventing you from creating what you truly want. You tell your secrets for your benefit, not necessarily for the benefit of your partner.

However, it is an important step to *intimacy* that you make an agreement between you and your partner to do this work. This action serves both parts of *intimacy*, *vulnerability* and *safety*. As the two of you approach the decision to create a conscious relationship, this is an agreement that will take considerable forethought. Each of you should approach the subject and discuss it thoroughly, but not make a choice until you have had a chance to feel about it and come to a deeper personal truth. Do not make an agreement, to clean up the past and not keep secrets, when you know full well that you intend to never speak about certain things. That would create yet another deception.

You cannot lie and live in truth. And you cannot keep secrets and live in truth. The only choice left is to be fully disclosing to your partner, with whom you are beginning a path of *intimacy*. When you feel ready to do whatever it takes to create real *intimacy,* you can make such an agreement in truth.

This agreement is one that is usually made after a relationship

---

[15] Keyes, ibid.

has gone through the attraction and romance stages, and is somewhere in the power struggle. This makes the agreement doubly important. Both of you must first deal with your *commitment* to create a conscious relationship, one which is founded in your personal truths. It is only after this is firmly established that you can begin to create the sense of *safety* about your partner necessary for you to choose such *vulnerability*. Before you *trust* in this mutual commitment to growth, you would probably maintain a certain level of *suspicion* about your partner's motivations. You might have difficulty believing they would never use any information against you in a moment of *anger* or *retribution*, and maybe rightly so.

The dance of *intimacy* is one that requires two willing partners. As a way of assuring yourself enough *safety* to allow you to deal with your deepest *vulnerabilities*, make sure you have agreement about what dance you and your partner are doing. If your partner is reluctant to agree to such a focused and *ambitious* endeavor, then you are left wondering about the level of *safety* present in your relationship. While there is a stage of growth where there is value in choosing *vulnerability,* even in the absence of *safety*, you would not be doing the dance of *intimacy*. If *intimacy* is what you are pursuing, deal with your experience of *safety* first; then choose *vulnerability*. Dynamics first, content second.

---

## INTIMACY <= SAFETY + **VULNERABILITY**

---

Like *safety*, *vulnerability* is an emotional experience. It is not a statement about your worth. Nor is it the condition of helplessness. *Vulnerability* is the continuous state of willingness to feel, and willingness to share your feelings with your partner. For example, if you feel *sad*, being *vulnerable* would be to acknowledge your *sadness* and to honestly express your *sadness*, instead of denying or avoiding it or expressing it as *anger, cynicism, mockery*, or any other of the many ways people often cover up their feelings.

To be *vulnerable* is to be as fully aware of your inner experience as you possibly can. It is allowing your emotions to be what they are, at any given moment. Instead of trying to cover up what you feel with something else that you imagine is more *acceptable,* you are willing to fully feel the emotions you have, at whatever intensity they occur. It is having your emotional power at full force, hardly a condition of helplessness.

When you are in a state of emotional *vulnerability*, being emotionally real, you are able to present your truest state of BEing. This facilitates your emotional exploration, and subsequent discovery of higher truth. Since you do not need to wade through one or more layers of cover-up emotions to get to what you are really feeling, you are able to walk the Path of Emotion much faster. You can claim your personal truth, and consciously choose your behavior within fractions of a second. Living constantly in this state of *vulnerability* enables you to more easily live consciously, all the time.

Like *safety*, there are specific things you can do to make it easier to choose *vulnerability*. First and foremost, you can make the choice to be honest, fully honest, in all areas, at all times, with all people, 100%, no compromise. Choosing to be honest means you will speak what is true for you; no quibbling, no slanting, no shading of the truth. It also means the people around you might not *like* what you have to say. Speaking your truth invites them to deal with the reality of your emotions, and subsequently, their emotions. By living honestly you will encounter your issues easily and readily, usually in smaller bite-size pieces, rather than in *overwhelming* chunks.

Being honest does not require you to speak your mind at all times, nor does it give you license to give unsolicited feedback to those around you. Your thoughts and your feelings are very different. Be honest with your emotions. Be discerning about your thoughts, along with the rest of your behavior.

As a part of choosing to be honest, you must confront the choice to come clean about any secrets you may be harboring. As previously presented, this is usually done within the context of a primary romantic relationship. However, it is helpful to practice full openness everywhere you feel it is *appropriate*. Much of your personal defense system is built around protecting these secrets. When you release the secrets, you release all of the energy that was previously going into guarding them.

A secret can be as benign as not wanting to tell anyone about the candy bar you stole when you were twelve years old, or as monstrous as having committed serious crimes against other people. As you release yourself from the chains of these secrets, you also release an accompanying set of emotions. *Relief* results from the release. Then other emotions will arise, due to the various invitations you receive from the people around you.

If you committed crimes, either moral or statutory, you can

probably expect to receive some measure of *rejection*. You may even have to *suffer* consequences from these behaviors that have been long delayed. But cleaning up the garbage, that results from your secret being disclosed, is always going to be better than carrying the garbage around with you while maintaining the secret. You are usually your own worst critic. You cannot fool yourself into believing you are really the image you pretend to be, when deep inside you know the truth. Coming clean about secrets in your life releases you from this burden, and allows you to begin living in truth. This alone would be a worthy accomplishment for any lifetime.

Here is an example of a secret, and a suggestion for how to work it through so it no longer presents an obstacle to your living in truth.

■■■■■■■■■■■■■■■■■■■■■■■■■■■■■■■■■■■■■■■■■■■■■■■■■■■■■

### Sexual Secret

A common secret that adults of both genders tend to keep involves sexual acts during childhood. These can fall into many different categories, including but not limited to: individual sexual exploration; mutual sexual exploration of child-peers; older child using a younger child to explore sex; consistent sexual acts perpetrated by an adult on a child; and so on. These sexual acts can have different effects upon the child, some benign or even *pleasing*. Some have long-lasting *destructive* effects.

The degree to which sexual acts during childhood have a *destructive* effect seems to be determined by the discrepancy between the levels of responsibility of the people involved. Two children of the same age and level of personal responsibility, who share in mutual sexual exploration, do not usually experience *trauma* from this. The imprint is light. Whereas, when an adult perpetrates sexual acts upon a child, their respective levels of personal responsibility are so divergent that there is always a *destructive* effect imprinted in the unconscious of the child, and, surprisingly, the adult. This imprint creates a pathology that must be dealt with as an adult, when you are attempting to claim full self-responsibility and therefore, higher consciousness.

The severity of the *trauma* is established by this discrepancy in personal responsibility for the sexual acts. The imprint is minimal when responsibilities are equal, and maximized as the responsibilities become disproportionate. This creates a spectrum of *trauma*, which can affect you

.

later in life. The trauma is created by the disproportionate responsibility, not the level of *pain, discomfort, displeasure, fear,* or *terror,* the child experienced at the times of the sexual incidences.

A child's body can actually respond to sexual pleasure and simultaneously be imprinted from this *trauma.* This is what confuses many adults who experienced sexual acts as a child. They think that because they possibly *enjoyed* some parts of it, they have a burden of responsibility to carry. And when they are taught to believe that sexual acts as a child are immoral, they create the emotional experience of *guilt* about their pleasure. Add to this the emotional *terror* that is invited out in the child by the all-powerful adult perpetrator, who must terrorize the child in order to maintain the level of secrecy necessary for such acts to occur. Between the conflicting emotions of *pleasure, responsibility, guilt,* and *terror,* it is no wonder that adults who experienced sexual acts as a child try to hide this experience from others.

This pathology occurs regardless of whether you are the victim-child or the perpetrator-adult. More times than not, the adult-perpetrator was also a child-victim. Even those child-victims who do not become adult-perpetrators carry this pathology within them. They continue the secrecy. They struggle with the emotional *dissonance.* They cannot *love* themselves. And therefore, they are unable to *love* others. If they have children, they perpetuate abuse; only now it shows as emotional abuse, mental abuse, or spiritual abuse.

■■■■■■■■■■■■■■■■■■■■■■■■■■■■■■■■■■■■■■■■■■■■■■■■■■■

The first step in dealing with this pathology is to break the silence. The secrets must be told so that you no longer give them power over you. A primary romantic relationship, in which two partners have committed to their own growth into higher consciousness, is the perfect place to begin this disclosure. An agreement between you to not keep any secrets lays the foundation by committing to the creation of an entirely *safe* environment, and by committing to be 100% honest, starting by coming clean about any secrets. Also keep in mind that you can invite *safety* by keeping someone's confidence. Your partner's *vulnerability* is not yours to disclose.

Other things you can do to choose into greater *vulnerability* are:
- Work on your level of consciousness by taking on the lessons that are presented to you each day, each

moment, on whatever aspect they occur.
- Seek out your lessons on every aspect; especially those that you know are less developed. Do not stay in your *comfort* zone, of relying on what you already know, to try to escape a lesson when it presents itself.
- Work constantly to become continuously aware of your core issues. Learn to spot them as they show themselves in every situation, every moment.

Relationships occur on the emotional aspect. It is how you feel about each other that defines a relationship. By using the Path of Emotion, you can create a relationship that is based in consciousness; one that allows you to encounter, deal with and learn from your core issues; and that allows you, through the pursuit of *intimacy*, to *unite* with at least one other person.

All relationship problems occur as a result of confusion over who is responsible for what. When relationship problems do occur, return to the Path of Emotion to discover where you are missing responsibility for your behavior, your emotions, or your personal truth. Return to the work of consciousness on the emotional aspect, the central lesson of which is self-responsibility. If you and your partner can help each other to do this inner work, even though you may feel *anger* or *frustration* at each other in this moment, then your relationship is perfect.

## INTIMACY <= SAFETY + VULNERABILITY

▲

## Epilogue – Living In Truth

earning to live truthfully is the greatest challenge faced by every individual. It is what allows you to successfully deal with issues, to create what you truly want, and to have truly *meaningful* relationships that allow you to experience *intimacy.*

It is by living in accordance with your personal truth that you can claim full responsibility for all that you experience, all of your behavior, and all of your personal truth, and therefore rise in consciousness. BEing truthful leads you to the higher consciousness experiences of *unity* with another individual, thereby making it possible to create these experiences with all things, *union.*

It is in this path, known as The Way, you can become one with all creation. In so doing, by BEing truthful, and by learning the lessons that are presented to you on all four aspects of your BEing, that you will claim all seven levels of consciousness and the Enlightenment that was your birthright. The Path of Emotion: Willingness, Exploration, Claiming Personal Truth, Choosing Truthful Behavior; is nothing less than the pursuit of God, the holiest of work, the purpose of all life. Along the journey, which begins with willingness to feel, there is a lot of experience to be felt.

> *"Even in a minority of one,*
> *the truth is still the truth."*
> (Mohandas Gandhi)

▲

## Appendix A
## Emotional Vocabulary

*I* n order to begin to identify your emotional experiences you need to have an adequate vocabulary for emotions. Being able to describe your emotions as accurately as possible is essential to identify and consciously use this source of energy.

An emotion word will always make sense by completing the sentence, "I feel..." Emotions can be adjectives (e.g. "I feel *overjoyed!*"). Sometimes they are nouns (e.g. "I feel such a *void!*"). Sometimes they are a simile (e.g. "He feels *like a victim.*" "I feel *like a rock.*") Sometimes they are verbs or adverbs. The English language is not well designed as a tool for the pursuit of higher consciousness.

This is an exercise of reflection for you to gain an appreciation for the depth and quality of your emotional experience. As you read through this list, try to identify with each emotion. Discover the nuances between similar emotions. See which ones you can easily identify with. Then see which ones you do not allow within your conscious experience (i.e. deny). Which emotions do you use to mask others? Ask yourself why some of them are easier to accept than others. What are the messages you can remember receiving from your parents about each emotion? Which ones do you define as positive and which as negative?

If you identify emotion words that are not included in this list, the authors would appreciate you sending these words to them so that they can be included in the next edition of this list.

## Emotion Words

| A | amused | B | bursting |
|---|---|---|---|
| abandoned | angry | bad | bushed |
| abhor | annoyed | badly | butterflies |
| able | antagonized | baffled | **C** |
| abnormal | antagonizing | banished | calm |
| abused | anticipating | barbarous | cantankerous |
| acceptable | anxious | bashful | capable |
| accepted | apathetic | bawdy | captivated |
| accepting | apologetic | beaten | captivating |
| accomplished | appalled | beautiful | cared for |
| accused | appealing | benevolent | careless |
| aching | appeased | betrayed | caring |
| adamant | appreciate | bewildered | castrated |
| adequate | appreciated | biased | censored |
| admired | apprehensive | big | centered |
| admiring | approachable | bitter | certain |
| adored | approved | blamed | challenged |
| adventurous | approving | blaming | challenging |
| affectionate | ardor | blind | charmed |
| afraid | arrogant | bliss | charming |
| aggressive | articulate | blissful | cheated |
| agonized | ashamed | blown-away | cheerful |
| agonizing | assertive | boiling | cheery |
| agony | astounded | bold | childish |
| agreeable | at ease | bored | chivalrous |
| airy | at home | boring | chosen |
| alarmed | attacked | bothered | circumstantial |
| alert | attended to | boxed-in | civil |
| alienated | attentive | brave | civilized |
| alive | attracted | bright | clean |
| allied | attractive | brilliant | clear |
| alone | aversion | brittle | clever |
| aloof | awake | bubbly | closed |
| amazed | aware | bugged | cluttered |
| ambiguous | awed | bullied | cocky |
| ambivalent | awestruck | bummed | cold |
| amoral | awkward | buoyant | combative |
| amorous | | burdened | comfortable |

comforted
comforting
coming-
unglued
committed
communicative
compassion
compassionate
competent
competitive
compromised
compromising
concerned
condemned
confident
confined
confirmed
conflicted
confused
congenial
connected
conquered
conscientious
conscious
consistent
consoled
conspicuous
constrained
consumed
contaminated
contempt
contemptuous
content
contented
contradicted
contrary
contrite
controlled
controlling
cool

corrupted
corrupting
courageous
courteous
cowardly
crazy
creative
credited
crippled
critical
criticized
crowded
cruel
crushed
cuddled
cuddly
curious
cut-off
cynical

**D**

damned
dangerous
daring
dark
dashing
deceitful
deceived
deceiving
deep
defeated
defensive
deflated
degraded
dejected
delighted
delightful
delirious
denied
denigrated
denigrating

dependent
depressed
depressing
deprived
deserving
desirable
desire
desirous
despair
despairing
desperate
desperation
despised
destructive
detached
determined
deterred
detested
detesting
different
difficult
dignified
diminished
diminishing
directed
dirty
disabled
disagreeable
disappointed
disappointing
disappointment
disapproved
disapproving
disbelieved
disbelieving
discarded
disclosed
disconcerted
disconnected
disconsolate

discontent
discontented
discounted
discounting
discouraged
discouraging
discredited
discrediting
discrete
discriminated
discriminating
dis'd
disdainful
diseased
disenchanted
disengaged
disguised
disgusted
disharmonious
disharmony
disheartened
dishonest
disillusioned
disillusioning
disinclined
disintegrated
disjointed
disliked
disliking
disloyal
dismal
dismayed
dismissed
disobeyed
disobeying
disordered
disoriented
disowned
disowning
disparaged

disparaging
dispassionate
dispirited
displeased
displeasing
displeasure
dispossessed
disregarded
disregarding
dissatisfied
dissatisfying
dissonance
distinct
distinguished
distracted
distraught
distressed
distressful
distressing
distrustful
disturbed
divided
dogmatic
dominated
dominating
domineering
doubt
doubted
doubtful
doubting
down
downcast
downhearted
down-in-the-
dumps
drained
dramatic
dubious
dull
dumb

dutiful

**E**

eager
easy
easy-going
ecstasy
ecstatic
edgy
elated
elation
electrified
emasculated
embarrassed
embraced
embracing
empathetic
empathy
emptiness
empty
enchanted
enchanting
encompassed
energetic
energized
enervated
engaged
engulfed
engulfing
enjoyable
enjoyment
enlightened
enmity
enraged
entertained
entertaining
enthused
enthusiastic
entitled
entrusted
enviable

envied
envious
envy
essential
esteemed
estranged
ethical
evasive
exasperated
excited
exhausted
exhilarated
exhilarating
exhilaration
expectant
explosive
exposed

**F**

faithful
fake
familiarity
fantastic
fascinated
fascinating
fast
fatalistic
fatigued
fear
fearful
fearless
fed-up
feeble
feminine
fickle
fidgety
filled
finished
flaky
flattered
flexible

flighty
flirtatious
flustered
focussed
foolish
forced
forgiving
forlorn
fouled
found
fragmented
frail
frantic
free
friendly
frightened
frigid
frisky
frozen
frustrated
fucked
fulfilled
full
funny
furious
futile

**G**

gallant
gay
generous
gentle
giddy
giggly
giving
glad
gloomy
glorious
glum
good
graceful

gracious
grandiose
grateful
gratified
great
greedy
grief
grieved
grok
groovy
grouchy
grounded
grumpy
guarded
guilty
gullible
gutless

**H**

haggard
handsome
happy
harassed
hard
hard-pressed
harmonious
harmony
harsh
hate
hated
hateful
heady
healthy
heard
heartbroken
heartsick
heavenly
heavy
helpful
helpless
heroic

high
hollow
holy
homesick
honest
honorable
honored
honoring
hopeful
hopeless
horrible
horrified
hospitable
hostile
humiliated
humility
humorous
hurt
hypocritical

**I**

idolized
idolizing
ignoble
ignored
ill-mannered
illogical
imaginative
immature
immobilized
immoral
impassioned
impatient
impeded
imperfect
impolite
important
imposing
impotent
impregnable
impressed

impressive
in control
inadequate
inappropriate
incapable
incensed
inclined
incoherent
incompetent
inconsistent
indecisive
independent
indifferent
indignant
indiscreet
indomitable
indulgent
ineffectual
infatuated
inferior
inflated
inflexible
influenced
informed
infuriated
inhibited
insane
insecure
insensitive
insincere
inspired
inspiring
insulated
insulted
insulting
integrated
intelligent
intense
interested
interesting

intimacy
intimate
intimidated
intimidating
intolerant
intrusive
invalidated
invective
invincible
invisible
invited
inviting
involved
irrational
irrelevant
irreplaceable
irresistible
irresolute
irresponsible
irreverence
irritable
irritated
isolated
isolation

**J**

jazzed
jealous
jittery
jolly
jovial
joy
joyful
joyless
jubilant
judgment
judgmental
jumbled
just
justified

**K**

keen
kind
kindly
kinship
knowledgeable

**L**

ladylike
lamenting
large
lazy
lecherous
led
left-out
lethargic
light
lighthearted
likable
like
like a ...
liked
limp
listless
little
lively
loathed
loathing
loathsome
logical
lonely
loose
loss
lost
lovable
love
loved
loving
low
loyal
lust

lustful
lustrous
lusty

**M**

macha
macho
mad
magnanimous
malleable
manipulated
manipulative
manly
masculine
masochistic
mature
mean
melancholy
mellow
merciful
merry
miserable
miserly
mistrusting
misunderstood
modest
moody
moral
mortified
motivated
motivating
moved
murderous
mystical
mystified
mystifying

**N**

naked
nasty
natural
naughty

nauseated
necessary
needed
needy
negative
neglected
negotiable
neighborly
nervous
neutral
nice
noble
noticed
numb
nurtured
nurturing

**O**

obligated
obliged
obliging
obnoxious
observant
observed
off-centered
okay
omnipotent
open
opposed
optimistic
ordinary
overjoyed
overloaded
overloading
overwhelmed
owned

**P**

pain
pained
painful
pampered

panicky
paralyzed
paranoid
pardoned
pardoning
passion
passionate
passive
patient
patriotic
peace
peaceful
peeved
pensive
peppy
perceived
perceptive
perfect
perky
perplexed
persecuted
perseverant
persuasive
perturbed
perverse
pessimistic
petrified
phony
pissed
pitied
pity
plain
playful
pleasant
pleasantness
pleased
pleasing
pleasure
poised
polite

| | | | |
|---|---|---|---|
| popular | **R** | resistant | seething |
| positive | raped | resisted | self-centered |
| possessed | rapturous | resolved | self-conscious |
| possessive | rational | respect | self-doubt |
| powerful | ready | respected | self-indulgent |
| prejudice | real | respectful | selfish |
| prejudiced | reasonable | respecting | self-serving |
| prepared | recognized | responsible | sensitive |
| presentable | recognizing | responsive | sensual |
| pressured | reconciled | rested | sentimental |
| presumed | redeemed | restless | separate |
| presuming | redeeming | restrained | settled |
| presumptuous | reflective | revealed | sexual |
| pretentious | refreshed | revealing | sexy |
| pretty | regarded | reverent | shabby |
| prevented | regarding | revived | shaky |
| principled | regretful | rewarded | shallow |
| privileged | rejected | rewarding | shamed |
| productive | rejuvenated | rich | shameful |
| progressive | relating | right | sheepish |
| prohibited | relaxed | righteous | sheltered |
| prompt | relevant | rightful | shielded |
| prompted | reliable | rigid | shielding |
| prosperous | relief | rigorous | shitty |
| protected | relieved | romantic | shocked |
| protective | religious | rough | shocking |
| proud | reluctant | **S** | shunned |
| provoked | remorseful | sad | shut-out |
| punctual | removed | sadistic | shy |
| purposeful | repelled | safe | sick |
| puzzled | repentant | satiated | silly |
| **Q** | represented | satisfied | simple |
| qualified | repressed | satisfying | sincere |
| quarrelsome | repulsive | saved | sinful |
| quenched | rescued | scared | skeptical |
| quenching | rescuing | scarred | skepticism |
| questioned | resented | screwed | skillful |
| questioning | resentful | seasoned | slow |
| quiet | reserved | secure | sluggish |
| quivery | resigned | seductive | small |

smart
sneaky
sociable
social
soft
soiled
solicited
soliciting
solicitous
sophisticated
sorrow
sorrowful
sparkling
special
speechless
speedy
spiritual
spiteful
spoiled
spontaneous
sportsmanlike
spry
squeamish
stable
staid
steadfast
steady
stern
strange
stressed
strong
stumped
stunned
stupid
suave
subdued
successful
suffering
suicidal
sullen

sunshiny
superior
supported
supportive
suppressed
sure
surrender
susceptible
suspected
suspecting
suspicion
suspicious
swayed
sympathetic

**T**

tacky
tactful
talented
tamed
tangential
tarnished
taxed
tempted
tender
tense
tentative
tenuous
terrific
terrified
terror
terrorized
tested
thanked
thankful
thawed
thoughtful
thoughtless
threatened
threatening
thrifty

thwarted
tidy
tight
timid
tired
together
torn
torn-up
touchable
touched
trammeled
trapped
tried
troubled
true
trusted
trusting
trustworthy
truthful
turmoil
turned-on
twisted

**U**

ugly
ugly
un-(other
emotion)
unabashed
unable
unaccomplished
unaccountable
unaccustomed
unaffected
unarmed
unassailable
unassertive
unassuming
unattached
unattractive
unaware

unbearable
unbending
unbiased
uncanny
uncaring
uncentered
uncertain
unclean
unclear
uncomfortable
uncommitted
unconcerned
unconscionable
unconscious
uncouth
undaunted
underhanded
undermined
undermining
understanding
understood
undirected
uneasy
unentitled
unequal
unfailing
unfair
unfeeling
unfilial
unfinished
unfit
unhappy
unhealthy
unheard
unimaginative
unimportant
unimpressed
unimpressive
uninhibited
uninvited

uninviting
uninvolved
unique
united
unity
unknown
unlikable
unlovable
unloved
unmoved
unnatural
unneeded
unnoticed
unobservant
unobserved
unopposed
unpopular
unprincipled
unprivileged
unproductive
unprogressive
unprosperous
unprotected
unprotective
unprovoked
unreal
unreasonable
unrecognized
unrecognizing
unreconciled
unredeemed
unredeeming
unregretful
unrelenting
unrepentant

unrepresented
unresisting
unresolved
unresponsive
unrestrained
unromantic
unruly
unsafe
unsatisfied
unscrupulous
unsettled
unsociable
unsophisticated
unstable
unstressed
unsuccessful
unsupported
unsure
untactful
untalented
untamed
unthankful
untouchable
untroubled
untrue
untrusted
untrusting
untrustworthy
untruthful
unusual
unwanted
unwelcome
unwholesome
unwilling
unworthy

unyielding
up
uppity
upset
uptight
urbane
used
useless
usual

**V**

valiant
validated
valuable
vanquished
vengeful
venturous
vibrant
victimized
victorious
violated
violent
virile
visible
vital
void
vulnerability
vulnerable

**W**

wanted
warm
wary
washed-out
watched
watchful
weak

wealthy
wearied
weary
weepy
weird
welcomed
whiney
whole
wholesome
wide-awake
wild
willing
wise
wishful
witty
womanly
wonderful
worn-out
worried
worthless
worthy
wrong

**X**

**Y**

yearning
yielding
youthful

**Z**

zany
zealous
zestful
zippy

## What Is BTES?

**BE**ing There Enlightenment Systems is an organized and continuously emerging process for seeking, growing into, and realizing the ultimate expression of human BEing: enlightenment. This is realized through personal growth into higher consciousness, the work of a lifetime. The specific skills and tools of the process are aimed at addressing any one of the four aspects of BEing (physical, mental, emotional, spiritual), depending upon what is needed by the individual, determined by their present level of consciousness. The first area of personal growth work is usually on the emotional aspect.

Although seeking can begin at any time, emotional skills are usually sought when the individual feels a sense of *disharmony*, *discontent*, *disruption*, or *pain*. A professional counselor is the guide for learning such skills. For this reason, BEing There Enlightenment Systems is found in the telephone directory under the heading of "Counselors." Counseling is the gateway to the work of personal growth, consciousness.

BTES goes far beyond counseling, though. Emotional skills address only one aspect of BEing. People who seek counseling from BTES eventually learn that consciousness involves the advancement of skills on all four aspects; the focus always BEing on the aspect of least development. By addressing all four aspects, the individual is able to realize greater consciousness, and develop the skills to become a conscious creator of life.

At higher consciousness, the individual experiences a reality that differs from that created at previous levels of consciousness. Some of these differences are *desired*, such as more meaningful relationships. All of them bring forth the lessons needed for the next stage of growth.

BTES is a privately owned company; owned by Donna BE and Stephen BE, and is supported by a growing number of fellow seekers. Both Donna and Stephen hold Masters Degrees from the University of West Georgia (formerly known as West Georgia College), and are Licensed Professional Counselors by the State of Colorado. Donna BE attended the University of Florida (Gainesville, FL.) before her graduate work. Stephen BE attended the U.S. Air Force Academy (Colorado Springs, CO), and the University of Colorado (Boulder, CO) for undergraduate work, and the University of Northern Colorado (Greeley, CO) and the National College of Naturopathic Medicine (Portland, OR) for post-graduate work.

For information
about products and services,
about the philosophy of BTES,
or the specifics of its various divisions:

BEingThere.net
BEing There Retreats™
SpeakTrue Invitations™
BEing There Counseling™
BEing There Publications™
BEing There Consciousness Tools™

Please visit us at our website:
www.BTES.com,


or request a catalog
by writing, calling or sending e-mail
(see information on Copyright page).

## Order Form

To order additional copies of ***Feeling* Your Way Along,** complete and return this order form, or you can order from website, **www.BTES.com**.

Name: _____

Address: _____

City: _____ State: _____ Postal Code: _____

Country: _____

Tel. (day): _____Tel. (eve.): _____

e-mail: _____ Fax: _____

Method of payment:

____ Check #_____                    ____ Money Order #_____

____ Credit card: ___AMEX ____Discover ____Visa ____M/C

    Card Number: _____

    Name on card: _____ Exp. Date: _____

    Authorization (sign here): _____

| Qty. | BEing There Publication | $US/$Can. | Total |
|---|---|---|---|
| __ | *High – C Journal* (annual subscription) | $24.00/$30.00 | _____ |
| __ | *Feeling* Your Way Along (soft cover) | $14.95/$18.95 | _____ |
| __ | High–C Journal: Volumes I & II | $24.95/$29.95 | _____ |
| __ | High–C Journal: Volume III | $24.95/$29.95 | _____ |
| __ | Journal To Consciousness | $19.95/$24.95 | _____ |

Sub-Total: _____

S&H add $3.00 per book: _____

Colorado residents add 5% state tax: _____

Grand Junction residents add 2.75% tax: _____

**Total:** _____

Please allow 10 business days for delivery.

Thank you for your order.

For bulk or wholesale orders, please call: **1-800-598-0370**

**Send order to:**

BEing There Publications™
650 Main Street, Suite 2
Grand Junction, CO 81501   USA